242.1
Rob.

Y0-AQV-155

NEW
GROWTH

PARK CITY BAPTIST CHURCH
PARK CITY, KENTUCKY

New Growth:

what the Holy Spirit wants to do for you

James Robison

Tyndale House
Publishers, Inc.
Wheaton, Illinois

Scripture quotations used
in this book are taken
from the King James
Version unless otherwise
indicated. Other transla-
tions used include: *The
Living Bible* (TLB) and
the *New American
Standard Bible* (NASB).

Library of Congress
Catalog Card Number
78-63095
ISBN 0-8423-4670-8
Copyright © 1978 by
James Robison.
First printing,
November 1978.
Printed in the United
States of America.

CONTENTS
Preface

PREFACE

As I have preached the gospel from coast to coast, both on television and in areawide evangelistic crusades, I have become increasingly convinced that the modern Christian's greatest need is to know and understand more about the work of the Holy Spirit in his own life and in the world. This book is designed to help Christians acquire this better understanding, as well as to stimulate them to personally engage in deeper study of the glorious truths concerning the Third Person of the Trinity.

Some of my messages on the Holy Spirit were published earlier in two booklets. These were: *Holy Spirit Possessed* (dealing with the baptism and gifts of the Spirit); *Alive in the Spirit* (a series of messages on the filling and fruit of the Holy Spirit).

Major portions of these previously published messages have been incorporated into this book, along with additional insights, the objective being to furnish the committed Christian witness with a broad, inspiring perspective concerning his relationship with Christ through the presence of the Holy Spirit.

PART I
THE
HOLY
SPIRIT
IN THE
WORLD

ONE
WHO IS THE HOLY SPIRIT?

What does America need, what does the world need, to successfully confront the nation's and mankind's problems? To the Bible-believing Christian, the answer is obvious: the Holy Spirit.

Why didn't I just say Jesus Christ? In a sense I did. The Holy Spirit lives and works as a personal representative of Jesus Christ. The Bible refers to the Holy Spirit as "the Spirit of Christ" (Romans 8:9) and "the Spirit of his Son" (Galatians 4:6). The Holy Spirit is also referred to in the Scriptures as "the Spirit of God" (Genesis 1:2). The Bible says the Spirit indwells us, yet also refers to "Christ in you" (Colossians 1:27).

Father, Son, and Holy Spirit are one, yet three. This is the profound doctrine of the Trinity—one God in three Persons. The Holy Spirit is often referred to as the third Person of the Trinity.

A SPIRITUAL STRUGGLE

The Holy Spirit manifests Jesus Christ in the world today. Current world problems are the result of a spiritual struggle, and the Holy Spirit alone has power to deal with the human plight created by this struggle. Men and women are walking "According to the course of this world" (Ephesians 2:2). The remainder of that verse explains why they are walking according to that course. They are being directed by a spiritual personality, "the prince of the power of the air," "the spirit that now worketh in the children of disobedience." Take careful note of that wording. It exposes plainly the source of the human dilemma. That source is spiritual, a spirit being. The escape from that dilemma must then also be spiritual.

SATAN'S WORK

According to Scripture, there is a spirit now working—notice, *now* working—in the children of disobedience, in all who have not obeyed God by receiving his Son, Jesus Christ, as their Savior and Lord. The Bible tells us that the answer to the human problem is for the "spirit that now worketh" in men to be replaced by another Spirit, the Spirit of Christ. The Spirit of Christ is Jesus living his life in and through the lives of those who have come to him in faith.

The Bible also refers to the Holy Spirit as "the Spirit of truth" (John 16:13). The wisdom of God is truth. The wisdom, or thinking, totally of this world is untruth. The wisdom of God must replace the wisdom of this world before the human problem can be solved. And this process must begin with the replacement, in the lives of individual human beings, of the spirit of disobedience to God with the Spirit of obedience, the Spirit of Christ, the Holy Spirit.

In the Scripture verse we are discussing, the spirit

who is described as directing the lives of unbelievers and leading them into the course of this world is not an idle spirit. He is a busy person. He is working constantly.

THE HOLY SPIRIT'S WORK

The Holy Spirit also is a diligent worker. He has work to do, and he never ceases to do it. That work is to continue the work of Jesus in the world.

Creation. A most important work of the Holy Spirit is that of creation. When God created the physical universe, the Spirit of God was an agent of new life. "The Spirit of God moved upon the face of the waters" (Genesis 1:2). But the Holy Spirit is involved even more directly in creation, so far as man is concerned. Job said, "The Spirit of God hath made me, and the breath of the Almighty hath given me life" (33:4). That reminds me of the title of a book by one of my Christian brothers: *It Takes God to Make a Man.* God didn't stop making men and women when he made Adam and then took a rib from him to make Eve. The Spirit of God is still at work creating men and women today.

To speak of the creative work of the Holy Spirit only in physical terms, however, would be to neglect the most miraculous aspect of his work in the world. The Holy Spirit not only makes men, but he also remakes them. In an object lesson taught to the prophet Jeremiah, the Lord used a potter to illustrate how he works in the lives of men. The potter fashioned a vessel, but discovered that it had become marred in his hand. So he molded the clay back into its original mass and started over, making it into another vessel "as seemed good to the potter to make it" (Jeremiah 18:4).

God is not pleased with man as he is in himself. He desires man to be spiritually alive, capable of having fellowship with a holy God. For that purpose, the Spirit of God keeps busy at his work of remolding and remaking men after his own image. The Spirit of God is a Spirit of renewal. As Isaiah explained to the Israelites, trouble is the lot of those who are in rebellion against God, and will be so "until the Spirit be poured upon us from on high, and the wilderness be a fruitful field, and the fruitful field be counted for a forest" (Isaiah 32:15). In other words, until the Holy Spirit does his work of renewal in us.

Before the Holy Spirit can do a work of renewal, remaking and recreating us as God would have us to be, he must perform another work, however. He must first break down the old creation. He must take the marred vessel and squash it into a submissive lump that he can work with. This work of the Holy Spirit is his all-important work of conviction.

Conviction. Jesus speaks of this ministry of the Holy Spirit in John 16:8-11: "And when he [the Holy Spirit] is come, he will reprove [or convict] the world of sin, and of righteousness, and of judgment: Of sin, because they believe not on me; of righteousness, because I go to my Father, and ye see me no more; of judgment, because the prince of this world is judged."

Conviction of Sin

What a fantastic, supernatural work the Holy Spirit performs in doing his work of conviction! The world frets and worries over its evil deeds. Though their efforts are spasmodic and largely ineffective, people actually try to correct their sins. But *sins* aren't the real problem. They are just symptoms. The real problem is *sin,* the sin nature. Sin is unbelief—unbelief in God and unbelief in Jesus

Christ, the One whom God has sent to take care of our problem of evil.

The Holy Spirit convicts people of wickedness. He convinces people that where they've actually gone wrong in life, and the reason they can't seem to put the pieces of their lives back together, is that they have refused to believe in God and to receive Jesus Christ as their personal Savior.

Before I turned my life over to Christ, I suffered under crushing guilt about my sins. I knew I was doing a lot of things God didn't like. I knew that my mouth was saying things God didn't want it to say, that my mind was thinking thoughts that were displeasing to God. I knew my hands were doing things God didn't want me to do, and I knew that my feet were taking me places he didn't want me to go. I was acutely aware of sins in my life.

But before I could receive Christ, the old vessel had to be smashed. I had to be brought to the understanding that I was never going to make it on my own. I had to be made to realize that my real problem was that I was in rebellion against God, that I was refusing to obey him, and that I was rejecting his Son who had given himself for me. I had to be made to see what a worthless, hopeless lump of mud I was apart from Jesus Christ. Only when I saw this was I in a proper condition to receive Christ.

It's important, too, that no human being gave me this understanding. No preacher persuaded me, no deacon argued me into it, my mother didn't beg me into it, and my father didn't force me into it. It couldn't have happened in any of those ways, because conviction of sin is the work of the Holy Spirit. We Christians need desperately to remember that. Believers don't, and can't, do the work of the Holy Spirit. They can only be *used* by the Holy Spirit in the work he is doing.

Conviction of Righteousness

The Holy Spirit doesn't stop with merely convicting people about sin. He also convicts the world of righteousness. That is, he shows the world that there is such a thing as righteousness, available because of the sinless life of Jesus, his death as a payment of the penalty for sin, and his resurrection from the dead and ascension to the Father, where he continually makes intercession for all who believe in him.

It wasn't enough for me to know what a worthless wretch I was. If that were all the Holy Spirit had taught me, it would have plunged me into despair. I might have wound up committing suicide. But he went on to show me that righteousness was possible for me—even me—through the finished work of Jesus Christ.

That's the good news. We're undone by sin, we're broken, we're marred. But through the work of Christ God has provided a way to put us back together, and to make us a better vessel than we could ever be on our own.

Conviction of Judgment

Another aspect of the good news the Holy Spirit brings, through his work of conviction, is that through Christ God will deliver us from the punishment we deserve. A terrible judgment awaits the world of sin, the world of those who remain in rebellion against God. That judgment is demonstrated in that the prince of this world, Satan, already has been sentenced. Through his Word, God reveals the nature of his judgment. It's so terrible that the Lord can explain it to the human mind only as everlasting fire, outer darkness, eternal death. It awaits all who let themselves be taken in by Satan and reject the salvation of God through Christ. But

praise God—all who receive Christ are given
salvation. Only the Holy Spirit can convince the
flint-like human heart of a truth such as this.

Regeneration. Once the Holy Spirit completes his
work of conviction, he is ready to begin another
work, that of regeneration or spiritual creation.
"Unless you are born again," Jesus told the self-
righteous Pharisee Nicodemus, "you can never enter
the Kingdom of God." The Holy Spirit must take the
lump, once the old vessel has been crushed, and re-
create it into a new vessel, one that God can accept.
He remakes us, not into an earthly vessel as we were
before, but into a spiritual vessel. "Men can only
reproduce human life, but the Holy Spirit gives new
life from heaven," Jesus said (John 3:6, TLB). The
new birth is "of the Spirit," he said (John 3:8), and
Titus 3:5 confirms it: " . . . according to his mercy he
saved us, by the washing of regeneration, and
renewing of the Holy Ghost."

The Apostle Paul tells us (2 Corinthians 5:17) that
when we become Christians we become new
creatures; that is, new creations. God is preparing a
new heaven and a new earth—not marred by sin—
and he is creating, by the work of the Holy Spirit, a
new population to inhabit the new environment.

Destruction. In light of conditions in this present world,
though, there's one other work of the Holy Spirit that
calls for our attention and understanding. The Holy
Spirit not only remakes men to better equip them to deal
with their enemy, "the spirit that now worketh in the
children of disobedience," but he also does something
about that enemy. In Hebrews 2:14 God tells us that
Jesus died to "destroy him that had the power of
death, that is, the devil." And in 1 John 3:8 he says,
"For this purpose the Son of God was manifested,

that he might destroy the works of the devil." This is
the Holy Spirit's work of destruction, for Christ
acted in the power of the Spirit.

To destroy, in the sense meant in these verses, is
not to obliterate. It doesn't mean that the devil has
been wiped out, completely expunged from existence.
It means, though, that his power over us has been
broken by the death of Jesus. He can no longer force
the born-again Christian to follow the course of this
world, rejecting the guidance of the Holy Spirit. By
the manifestation—that is, the revealing—of Jesus,
the Son of God, the works of the devil are destroyed.

Just think what this means. In Ephesians 2:2 the
devil is revealed as working feverishly to lead
mankind away from God. First John 3:8 reveals that
by constantly revealing Jesus to men, the Holy Spirit
is working to undo this work of Satan and to lead
men to salvation through Christ.

Here, however, is the part that both thrills and
challenges me. The Holy Spirit uses us in his work of
bringing men and women to Christ. We are
communication channels for the Holy Spirit.

THE SPIRIT'S INSTRUMENTS

The Bible tells us that God has chosen Christians
to be instruments through whom the Holy Spirit will
perform his work of conviction, renewal, and the
undoing of the work of Satan. As God sent Jesus into
the world (to seek and to save that which was lost,
according to Luke 19:10), so he has sent us into the
world (John 20:21).

How well are we performing as instruments,
Christian brothers and sisters? Are we really yielding
ourselves to God, to be used of him in the soul-
saving work he is doing? Or are we, through
indifference or disobedience, hindering his work?

The Scriptures warn us to "grieve not the Holy Spirit" (Ephesians 4:30). We grieve the Holy Spirit, I believe, when we do anything that makes us ineffective as instruments in his service.

The Scriptures also warn us not to "quench" the Holy Spirit (1 Thessalonians 5:19). When we rebel against the instructions of the Holy Spirit by not obeying his pleas to seek time alone with God every day for fellowship, Bible study, and prayer, we quench his work in us. Some are quenching the Spirit by not surrendering to his urgings to commit their lives for witnessing, teaching, or some other responsibility in the church or in their daily lives.

This is resisting the Holy Spirit in one's own life, but Christians also can hinder the Holy Spirit in the lives of other Christians, or even non-Christians. Church members who are hateful or uncooperative with their pastors are quenching the Holy Spirit in their pastors. They are making it difficult for their pastors to be as effective instruments of the Holy Spirit as they might be. Christians can quench the Holy Spirit in their fellow church members with acts of jealousy, backbiting, selfishness, and pettiness. Many a young believer has stumbled over the childish, immature behavior of some church members.

If your life is yielded to the Holy Spirit's control, the Holy Spirit can reveal Christ to others through you. If you're not yielded, you're quenching the Holy Spirit. You're interfering with the work he is trying to do in the hearts of believers and unbelievers with whom you come in contact as you live your life.

PART II
THE
HOLY
SPIRIT
IN THE
CHURCH

TWO
SWAYBACKED CHRISTIANS

In a small Texas town some time ago, there lived an
old man who scavenged for his living. He would
wander the alleys, searching through junk and trash
that people had thrown away for items that might be
salvaged and sold. His only help and only companion
was the mare that pulled his squeaky old wagon.

I don't remember much about the old man, but I'll
never forget that horse. I have never seen a more
swaybacked creature. She was tall and straight in
the front and again in back, but in between she had
the roller-coaster look. If her back had swept any
lower, she would have needed a wheel underneath to
keep her middle from dragging on the ground. I used
to watch her—laboring along in front of that wagon,
her head bobbing grotesquely up and down with
every step she took—and I'd wonder when she would
finally collapse at midpoint and crash to earth,
leaving her four legs to topple in on her like two
spindly pairs of stilts.

THE MISSING LINK

What causes a horse to become swaybacked? The bones in the legs are big and strong, and they deteriorate relatively slowly with age. But the spine is only a thin row of joints held together by muscle and soft gristly material. When the muscles and other tissues give way because of age or overwork, the spine sags.

The world is full of Christians like that. Healthy in back and front, but no backbone! Sturdy in back—in the past, that is—because they have trusted Christ as the Savior whose death has atoned for their past sins. Sturdy in front—in the future—because they believe in Christ as the Savior who has gone on to prepare a place for them and will come again to receive them unto himself. But weak in the middle—in the here and now. Sagging and defeated in their moral and present spiritual lives because they are not relying on Christ to be their source of strength for a pure and fruitful life moment by moment and day by day.

When a horse becomes swaybacked, about all it's good for is to pull a junk wagon. It's too slow to be a range horse, used to help control herds of cattle. It lacks the courage and stamina to be a cavalry pony, charging into the thick of battle. With its puny back, it can't even be used as a beast of burden or a plow-horse.

A swaybacked Christian is equally as ineffective. He can produce little that is noble, praiseworthy, or pleasing in the sight of God. How could he? By his failure to depend on Christ as Savior here and now, as the source of his everyday life, he has forsaken what God has provided to enable him to live a life pleasing to God.

Remember Jesus' words "I am the vine, ye are the branches...without me ye can do nothing"? Not "pretty well," not "just a little." *Nothing.* That means that without him we can't save ourselves from our past guilt, we can't get into heaven beyond the grave—and we can't live this present life in a manner that honors and pleases God!

A DOCTRINAL VIRUS

What produces swaybacked Christians? It's the doctrinal virus that says, "Yes, a Christian is saved by the grace of God when he accepts Christ as Savior; but once saved he must strive in his own power—out of gratitude and sincerity—to live a life that pleases God." It's the doctrine that is summed up in the familiar phrase, "God helps those who help themselves."

That's the doctrine that I've come to call "Satan's big lie." It's the devil's lie to the church of Jesus Christ, in order to rob the church of supernatural power. It's the lie he tells the Christian, whom Christ has freed from slavery to sin, in order to keep him from being an effective servant of God.

Dictators have been able to bring great nations under subjection by shouting one big lie so loud and so often that the people finally began to believe it. And Satan, the cleverest dictator the world has ever known, has deceived much of the church of God down through the ages, just by repeating this one big lie over and over to generation after generation of Christians.

AN ANCIENT DISEASE

Swaybacked Christians aren't a new breed. Paul wrote to whole churches of them in Galatia 1,900 years ago. "O foolish Galatians," Paul said, "who hath bewitched you, that ye should not obey the

truth..." (3:1). And what is the truth? That the just
are not only *saved* by faith, but they also *live* by
faith after they've been saved. That the law of God is
fulfilled in Christ, and that Christ—the law
personified—is given to every one who believes in
him. That Christians please and glorify God as they,
in simple faith, let Christ live his life in and through
them.

But some emissaries of Satan had slipped into the
midst of these Galatian believers to spread the big
lie. "You were right in accepting Jesus as the sacrifice
for your sins," they said, "but now in order to please
God, you must observe all the rules and rituals of the
Jewish religion."

Paul exposed the folly of this doctrine when he
asked the Galatians, "Are ye so foolish? having
begun in the Spirit, are ye now made perfect by the
flesh?" (3:3). The *New American Standard Bible*
states the case Paul was making in those first four
verses of Galatians 3, " . . . did you receive the Spirit
by the works of the Law, or by hearing with faith?
Are you so foolish? Having begun by the Spirit, are
you now being perfected by the flesh? Did you suffer
so many things in vain—if indeed it was in vain?"

A HEAVEN-SENT CURE

Many Christians in Galatia had believed Satan's
big lie. So have many others through the ages. And
today only a relatively small handful of persons, out
of all the millions who call themselves Christians,
have resisted Satan's big lie and appropriated the
resources of the indwelling Christ in living their
Christian lives.

In the remainder of this book, I want to talk about
how Christians receive the Holy Spirit and the
provisions he makes for them to have lives that

honor and please God. This is a book dedicated to the cure of swaybacked Christians—pointing them to the One who can give them the backbone they need.

THREE
THE BAPTISM
OF THE HOLY SPIRIT

In his letter to the church at Corinth, Paul was
writing to one of the weakest, puniest groups of
Christians found anywhere during the New
Testament age. The congregation was riddled with
sin. There was envy and factionalism among the
believers, some claiming to be superior to others
because they had been baptized by Peter, Paul, or
Apollos. There was drunkenness—even during the
observance of the Lord's Supper! There was
immorality of such a disgusting type that not even
the idol-worshipers of the surrounding pagan
community would be guilty of it.

To these spiritually frail and sickly Christians,
Paul put a very thought-provoking question. Out of
sheer exasperation he asked: "Or do you not know
that your body is a temple of the Holy Spirit who is
in you, whom you have from God, and that you are
not your own?" (1 Corinthians 6:19, NASB).

And the same question could be asked of
multitudes of powerless Christians today: "Haven't
you yet learned this basic, fundamental fact of your
faith—that the Holy Spirit, your means of living a

life pleasing to God, lives in you, right now?" And in answer many would say, "I thought that was just poetic language, to encourage me to do my best for the Lord." Others would say, "I know some Christians have the Holy Spirit, but I'm just not that holy." Others: "The Holy Spirit was for the early church, not for us." And still others: "I don't have the Holy Spirit yet, but I'm praying to receive him."

The fact that so many would give one or another of these answers to Paul's simple question explains why the church stands bewildered and trembling amid the evils of the modern world. For to know and believe the written Word of God is to realize that the Holy Spirit lives in every believer from the moment he is born into the family of God. Not to realize this is to live a weak and defeated life, as did the Corinthians to whom Paul wrote.

ALIVE IN EVERY CHRISTIAN

Speaking of an age to come (our own age?) Isaiah prophesied that the Spirit would be "poured upon us from on high" (32:15) and voiced God's promise, "I will pour my Spirit upon thy seed, and my blessing upon thine offspring" (44:3). In Joel 2:28 God promised that the time would come when he would pour out his Spirit on "all flesh." And when the Holy Spirit descended on the believers at Pentecost, Peter quoted Joel's prophecy and declared that this was the event of which the prophet had spoken. From these verses, and numerous others, it's clear that the Holy Spirit, one of the three Persons of the Trinity, is given to believers today. And he is given to "all flesh"—all, that is, whom God has redeemed through his Son, Jesus Christ. The Holy Spirit isn't reserved for the pastor, the teacher, or the super-saint. He lives in every believer.

The Scriptures make this point plain in a number of truths they reveal. Let's examine some of these truths.

Jesus' Two-fold Work. The two-fold work of Jesus in the life of the believer is clearly delineated in the first chapter of John. In verse 29, John the Baptist announces one aspect of Jesus' work, the one most familiar to the majority of Christians: "Behold the Lamb of God, which taketh away the sin of the world." Praise God—Jesus has paid the penalty for your sin and mine. He has blotted out our sin with his precious blood.

But now look at the second facet of his work described in verse 33. John the Baptist is speaking again, and he says: ". . . He that sent me to baptize with water, the same said unto me, Upon whom thou shalt see the Spirit descending, and remaining on him, the same is he which baptizeth with the Holy Ghost." The second part of Jesus' two-fold work in the believer is to baptize him with the Holy Spirit.

The first part of Jesus' work is negative, the second positive. In the first part, he is putting away sin. In the second part, he is putting in the Holy Spirit. The first part leaves the sinner clean in the sight of God. But as Romans 8:10 says, "the Spirit is life." Without the entrance of the Holy Spirit into the believer, there could be no life. The new birth would be incomplete. In this light, read those familiar but so commonly misunderstood words in Titus 3:5: Yes ". . . according to his mercy he saved us, by the washing of regeneration, and renewing of the Holy Ghost." Here the two-fold work of Jesus is plainly restated. He saves us by (1) a rebirth that cleanses us and (2) the Holy Spirit who renews us. The incoming of the Holy Spirit is part of the two-fold process by which Jesus saves.

No wonder Paul could say, "If any man have not
the Spirit of Christ, he is none of his" (Romans 8:9).
If you're saved, you have the Holy Spirit. If you don't
have the Holy Spirit, you're not saved.

Conditions Fulfilled. Like all of God's promises, his
promise to place his Spirit in the hearts of men
comes with conditions attached. God doesn't pour out
his Spirit on all humanity. To receive the Holy Spirit,
a person must fulfill God's requirements. The
conditions for receiving the Holy Spirit are clearly
stated in his written Word.

While Peter was explaining the outpouring of the
Spirit on the believers at Pentecost, his non-Christian
listeners were "pricked in their heart." The Holy
Spirit was doing his work of conviction on them as
the apostle spoke. And they interrupted him with a
question framed in the depths of their guilt-ridden
misery: "What shall we do?"

Two problems burdened them. They were suddenly
conscious of the sinfulness that saturated their
nature, resembling the venom of a poisonous snake.
And they were conscious of the new nature evident
in the believers whom they had mocked and
ridiculed.

"What shall we do?" The apostle, filled with the
Holy Spirit, answered clearly and straight to the
point: "Repent, and be baptized every one of you in
the name of Jesus Christ . . ." (Acts 2:38).

There you are—God's two conditions. First,
repent—change your mind and your attitude toward
your sin, forsake it, turn away from it. Second, be
baptized in the name of Jesus Christ—plunge yourself
into Christ, depending completely on him for your
salvation.

And to all who would fulfill these conditions, God
made two promises. Look at the rest of Acts 2:38:

". . . for the remission of sins, and ye shall receive
the gift of the Holy Ghost." In *The Living Bible* this
reads: ". . . for the forgiveness of your sins; then you
also shall receive this gift, the Holy Spirit."

Does that sound familiar? It should. For it's merely
another statement of the two-fold work of Christ in
the believer: remission of sin and the reception of the
Holy Spirit.

In reality, the two conditions and the two promises
are one. It would be impossible for a believer to
fulfill one condition and not the other. Why? Because
there's really only one way to turn from sin, and
that's to turn to Christ. "Whatsoever is not of faith
[in Christ] is sin" (Romans 14:23). By the same token,
it would be impossible for a believer to receive one of
the promises without receiving the other. Would Jesus
perform the first part of his work, then leave the
cleansed vessel to the ravages and defilement of
Satan? Hardly. He said, "I will not leave you
comfortless: I will come to you" (John 14:18).

Every believer—that is, everyone who has come
under conviction of sin and has accepted Christ as
Savior—has received not only God's gift of
forgiveness but also his gift of the Holy Spirit,
because every such believer has fulfilled the
conditions God placed on these promises.

Promise and Call. There is further scriptural proof
in Acts 2:39 for the exciting fact that every believer
receives the Holy Spirit the moment he or she
believes.

Peter, referring both to remission of sins and to
God's gift, the Holy Spirit, said, "For the promise is
unto you, and to your children, and to all that are
afar off, even as many as the Lord our God shall
call."

What a marvelous thing this is! Nobody gets left

out. If you're included in God's call, you're included in his promise of forgiveness and baptism with the Holy Spirit. You don't have to be a deacon, or a preacher, or an evangelist, or a Sunday school teacher. If you can count yourself among those who have been called by God to salvation through Christ Jesus, you can be certain, on the basis of God's own Word, that your sins have been removed and that the Holy Spirit lives in you.

The promise and the call are inseparable. The promise is made to all who are called.

Taken for Granted. Time and again, the men whom God chose to write the books of the New Testament took it for granted that God has given his "gift of the Spirit" to every believer. The Scripture verses that show this are numerous.

By the Apostle Paul:
Paul's writings were filled with remarks assuming that all of his Christian readers possessed the Holy Spirit. In Romans 5:5, he referred to the "love of God . . . shed abroad in our hearts by the Holy Ghost which is given unto us" (unto himself and all the Christians at Rome). In 2 Corinthians 13:5, he exhorted all the Corinthian believers to "examine yourselves, whether ye be in the faith," and then put them to the ultimate test with the question: "Know ye not your own selves, how that Jesus Christ is in you, except ye be reprobates?" In other words, "Unless you have the Holy Spirit living in you, you're not a Christian at all; you're a phony."

When Paul discovered evidence that persons he thought to be Christians did not possess the Holy Spirit, he reacted with astonishment. I've already mentioned 1 Corinthians 6:19, in which the apostle asked in shocked disbelief: "Haven't you yet learned that the Holy Spirit lives in you, right now?"

The classic example of this is in Acts 19:1-6. At Ephesus, Paul found a group of disciples whom he at first assumed to be Christians. He asked them—and all competent language scholars now agree that this is the correct translation of his words—"Did you receive the Holy Spirit when you believed?" Obviously something they said or did had caused him to wonder. Their reply confirmed his suspicions. "No," they said, "we don't know what you mean. What is the Holy Spirit?" Paul knew then that they could not be Christians, so he asked, "Unto what then were ye baptized?" And they said, "Unto John's baptism"—the doctrine of repentance preached by John the Baptist.

Paul immediately explained that John merely prepared the way for the Savior, Jesus Christ, who was to come after him—and indeed had come. As soon as they heard this, they were baptized in the name of the Lord Jesus. And when Paul laid his hands on them, no doubt in the baptismal process, the Holy Spirit came on them. Of course he did! They were now born again. They had not only repented of their sins, they had experienced the two-fold work of Christ—forgiveness of sins and the giving of the Holy Spirit.

By the Lord Himself:
Jesus himself assumes that all believers receive his Holy Spirit the moment they believe. In John 14:18 he promises, "I will come to you." He continues, in verse 20, saying, "At that day ye shall know that I am in my Father, and ye in me, and I in you." Notice, "at that day" (the day Jesus comes to the believer), the believer is expected to know that Jesus is in him.

Further, Jesus, as we see by his constant use of the word "abide," expects every believer to understand this truth. "Abide in me, and I in you." The word means simply "to stay or remain." I doubt that Jesus would command us to let him "abide" (stay) in us if he were not already in us. If one of my children were outside the house and I wanted him inside, I might tell him to "get in the house and stay there." But I wouldn't just say, "Stay in the house." And that, in everyday language, is all Jesus says: "You stay in me; I will stay in you." Plainly the Lord meant for us to understand that we have already entered into him and he into us when we believed. Otherwise, he would have talked about entering, not staying.

By the Apostle John:
First John 4:15 says, "Whosoever shall confess that Jesus is the Son of God, God dwelleth in him, and he in God." The truth of God's living presence in the heart of every believer could not be stated more clearly. God, by his Holy Spirit, lives in everyone who confesses that Jesus is the Son of God!

Confirmed by the Spirit. In addition to all the Scriptures that tell us about the Holy Spirit's presence in the life of every believer, God has given us another indisputable witness of the fact, the Holy Spirit himself. Writing to all the believers at Rome, Paul said (8:15,16): "For ye have not received the spirit of bondage again to fear; but ye have received the Spirit of adoption, whereby we cry, Abba, Father. The Spirit itself beareth witness with our spirit, that we are the children of God."

This is a tremendous fact for the Christian to know. But many Christians, though familiar with this verse, are still not sure they have received the baptism of the Holy Spirit. They are still not certain the Holy Spirit lives in them, and has since the moment they believed. The reason is really quite simple. They don't understand how the Holy Spirit speaks to them, how he bears witness to them of his presence with them.

He does it in numerous ways, but we'll talk about just a few. Again, our source will be the written word of God.

The Evidence of Peace:

Jesus gives us the first clue to receiving the witness of the Holy Spirit, confirming his presence within us. Appearing to the disciples after his resurrection, the Lord said, ". . . Peace be unto you: as my Father hath sent me, even so send I you. And when he had said this, he breathed on them, and saith unto them, Receive ye the Holy Ghost" (John 20:21, 22).

The Holy Ghost was not given until later, on the Day of Pentecost. But Jesus had given the disciples their instructions to receive him, and he had given them the sign by which they would know him— peace.

Think back to the moment you put your faith in Jesus Christ. What was the first change you were aware of in your heart? Wasn't it a great sense of peace? Wasn't it a joyous realization that your burden of sin was lifted and that now, through the blood of Jesus, you were reconciled to God? And didn't you sense not only this marvelous peace with God, but also with your fellowman? That was the Holy Spirit speaking to you in his spiritual language. That was his quiet, reassuring voice saying, "Peace be unto you." For he always brings to our remembrance the things Jesus has said. "Lo, I am with you, not just in this wonderful moment, but always—unto the end of the age."

The Evidence of Revealed Truth:

Remember some of the other things Jesus said about the Holy Spirit. "He shall teach you all things" (John 14:26). "He will guide you into all truth . . . and he will show you things to come" (John 16:13).

Do you recall how just after you received Christ, Scriptures you had never been able to make heads or tails of suddenly sprang to life? Passages that had no meaning for you at all began to leap out at you with truths that thrilled your heart. And even now, no matter how long you've been a believer, aren't you sometimes startled by flashes of spiritual revelation that illuminate your heart? That's the Holy Spirit confirming his presence within you.

You can be certain of this, because without the Holy Spirit living within you there would be only three spiritual truths you could know: (1) that you were a sinner, (2) that righteousness was possible for you only through Christ, and (3) that judgment awaits all who reject his righteousness (John 16:9-11). Aside from these three things, God's spiritual truths are incomprehensible to the man in whom the Holy Spirit does not live. And even these three things would remain unknown to him except for the fact that the Holy Spirit is committed to reveal just that much to the lost man, that he might know enough to be saved. "Eye hath not seen, nor ear heard, neither have entered into the heart of man, the things which God hath prepared for them that love him" (1 Corinthians 2:9). "The natural man receiveth not the things of the Spirit of God; for they are foolishness unto him," says verse 14 of the same chapter. But look at that precious verse 10: "But God hath revealed them unto us by his Spirit."

What a tremendous truth for every believer to feast on! As it says in still another wonderful verse in that

chapter, verse 12: "Now we have received, not the
spirit of the world, but the Spirit which is of God;
that we might know the things that are freely given
to us of God." And the fact that we can know these
things is in itself a powerful testimony from the Holy
Spirit that he lives within us to do the work he has
been sent by the Father to perform.

The Holy Spirit bears witness to us in countless
other ways, but let's look at just two other important
ones.

The Evidence of Victory:

In 1 John 4:4 we are told: "Ye are of God,
little children, and have overcome them (Satan's
deceivers and false teachers): because greater is he
that is in you than he that is in the world." Have you
been able to overcome temptations and sins since you
trusted Christ? If you've mastered one sin or resisted
one lure of the tempter, that was evidence of the
Holy Spirit in you. For only he is "greater than he
that is in the world." Without him you would be
powerless before the forces of Satan and your evil
human nature.

The Evidence of Love:

The Holy Spirit also bears witness to us by
filling our hearts with a love that is foreign to our
old human nature. "The love of God is shed abroad in
our hearts by the Holy Ghost which is given unto us"
(Romans 5:5).

"Love is of God" (1 John 4:7), not of this world,
"and he that dwelleth in love dwelleth in God, and
God in him" (1 John 4:16).

Anyone who experiences genuine, self-giving love
can, by the authority of God's Word, interpret this
love as a testimony from the Holy Spirit that he has
taken up residence in him. For only the Holy Spirit,

who is given unto us who believe, is able to produce
and increase such love in our hearts.

BAPTISM OF THE SPIRIT:
WHAT DOES IT MEAN?

We've looked at some Scriptures testifying that all
Christians receive the Holy Spirit when they believe.
Perhaps we can better understand this experience if
we delve deeper into the meaning of the expression
"baptism of the Holy Spirit."

The first thing to note is that the term "baptism" is
initiatory in its very concept. It connotes the very
beginning of something. When we say a soldier has
received his baptism under fire, we mean that he has
tasted battle for the first time and has begun his
combat career. Every Christian understands water
baptism as an initiatory rite. Every Christian sees
water baptism at least as a beginning of a
relationship with the church.

The fact is—and not all Christians realize this—
that this water baptism should be the symbol of
Spirit baptism, which is the reality. One passage of
Scripture bears this out with greater force than
perhaps any other. When Cornelius and his
household heard the gospel, they believed and
immediately received the Holy Spirit. Seeing this,
Peter said, in effect, "Can anyone forbid water for
baptizing these people who have received the Holy
Spirit just as we have?" Why should anyone deny
these new Christians the symbol when they
obviously had already experienced the reality?

The Four Agents. But let's analyze the baptism of the
Holy Spirit still further. John R.W. Stott, a leading
British Bible scholar, points out that this phrase
appears seven times in the New Testament. Four of
the seven record the prophecy of John the Baptist in

the Gospels (Matthew 3:11; Mark 1:8; Luke 3:16; John 1:33). The fifth is Jesus' quotation of John's prophecy (Acts 1:5), applying it to Pentecost. The sixth is in Acts 11:16, where Peter quoted the Lord's quotation of John the Baptist. The seventh is in 1 Corinthians 12:13, where Paul stressed the experience of the Holy Spirit as common to all Christians.

In every kind of baptism, Dr. Stott points out, there are four factors: a baptizer, the baptized, an element with or in which the baptizing is done, and finally a purpose. Thus, in John's baptism John was the baptizer; the people "of Jerusalem and all Judea," etc., were the baptized; the element was the water of the Jordan River; and the purpose was for repentance (Matthew 3:11) and therefore remission of sins (Mark 1:4; Luke 3:3).

Now let's see how our four agents apply in the seven verses referring to the baptism of the Holy Spirit. In all seven instances, Jesus Christ is the baptizer, the person accepting Christ as Savior and Lord is the baptized, the Holy Spirit is the "element" into which the person is baptized, and the purpose is to incorporate the baptized into "one body," the body of Christ, and to empower that person to fulfill the will of God in his life.

Translations of the original language vary considerably. But the original is the same in each of the seven references. On the basis of the original wording, the common phrase should be not "baptism of the Holy Spirit" but "baptism with (or in) the Holy Spirit." John the Baptist baptized with water. But his prophecy was that the One who came after him would baptize "with the Holy Spirit, and with fire." Pentecost was the initial fulfillment of that prophecy.

The Beginning Experience. Baptism with the Holy Spirit is the beginning of the Christian life. It is the means by which one is incorporated into the body of Christ. It's the believer's first experience of the spiritual life. Since baptism with the Spirit is the only way to become a Christian, then it follows that anyone who is a Christian has experienced baptism with the Holy Spirit and has the Holy Spirit living in him.

What a tragedy that this vital truth of the Christian faith is misunderstood or rejected by so many Christian believers today.

BAPTISM OF THE SPIRIT: WHAT IS THE EVIDENCE?

Why do so many Christians fail to realize that their salvation experience not only includes a baptism with the Spirit, but actually depends on such a baptism? This is primarily due to preconceived ideas that many people have concerning what the baptism with the Spirit should be like.

In the minds of many, Spirit baptism should always resemble the events of the day of Pentecost. But this was no more a typical baptism with the Spirit than Paul's conversion was a typical conversion. Must every baptism with the Spirit be accompanied by wind, fire, and speaking in tongues? It would be just as logical to insist that every conversion must be accompanied by blinding light and a voice from heaven. The events at Pentecost and on the Damascus Road were supernatural, outward accompaniments of an inward experience. God had a purpose in sending thesse dynamic manifestations, but the outward signs were not a necessary part of what was going on in the heart.

Special Manifestations. The Bible doesn't support the idea that speaking in tongues is a necessary sign of baptism with the Spirit. Many groups and individuals are recorded in Acts as having received the Spirit, but only three are said to have spoken in tongues. And in each of these instances, there were circumstances suggesting that God had special reason to give dramatic, visible, audible evidence to accompany his giving of the Spirit.

No one can deny that Acts 2:1-4 certainly recounts a special, nontypical experience. This was the initial fulfillment of "that which was spoken by the prophet Joel"(2:16), the pouring out of the Spirit upon "as many as the Lord our God shall call" (2:39). It was a dawning of a new age. It was the beginning of the "ministration [dispensation] of the spirit [Holy Spirit]," characterized by a law written in the heart of the believer (2 Corinthians 3:7, 8; Jeremiah 31:33).

In Acts 10:44-48, the setting is the home of Cornelius, the centurion. In this incident, Gentile believers were receiving baptism with the Spirit for the first time. God's purpose in sending the supernatural manifestation this time can be seen in the reaction of the Jews who were present: "And all the circumcised believers who had come with Peter were amazed, because the gift of the Holy Spirit had been poured out upon the Gentiles also. For they were hearing them speaking with tongues and exalting God. Then Peter answered, 'Surely no one can refuse the water for these to be baptized who have received the Holy Spirit just as we did, can he?' " (vv. 45-47, NASB). It's clear that God gave this sign to the Jews to convince them that Christ came not just for them, but for all the world.

Finally, in Acts 19:6 the "sign gift" of tongues was given to a group of twelve Jews at Ephesus. They had been disciples of John the Baptist who didn't even know there was any such person as the Holy Spirit. The outward manifestations were not only to emphasize to them how incomplete and inadequate their experience had been with only John's baptism, but to serve as a sign to the unbelieving Jews to whom Paul soon would be witnessing (vs. 8).

When we use these special incidents to picture in our minds what it's like to receive the Holy Spirit, we're almost certain to end up confused and deprived of the blessings that are rightfully ours.

The General Teaching. To avoid confusion and disappointment, we should stick to the general teaching of the New Testament in regard to this vital truth. The general teaching regarding reception of the Holy Spirit is plain. We receive the Holy Spirit "by believing the gospel message" (Galatians 3:2, James Moffatt translation)—in other words, "through faith" (Galatians 3:14). All of God's sons possess the Holy Spirit (Galatians 4:6), are led by the Holy Spirit (Romans 8:14), and are assured by the Holy Spirit of the fact that they are sons (Romans 8:15, 16).

The chief evidence of the Holy Spirit in our lives is the fruit of the Spirit, primarily love (Galatians 5:22, 23; Romans 5:5). When this evidence is weak or lacking, however, it isn't necessarily proof that a professing Christian is not really born again. It may simply mean that the individual is not filled with the Spirit; that is, not yielded to the Spirit's control. The Christians at Corinth had been baptized with the Spirit (1 Corinthians 12:13). Yet Paul called them "carnal"—i.e., unspiritual or, better still, un-Spirit-filled. The Scriptures never record anyone receiving a second baptism of the Spirit after their original conversion experience. But they recount numerous incidents of the same persons being filled again with the Spirit.

The Cause of Confusion. Paul's command to Christian believers in Ephesians 5:18 is not that they be baptized with the Spirit. Such a command would be nonsensical, since spiritual baptism is the initial, once-for-all event by which a person becomes a Christian. The command is to be *filled* with the Spirit or, more in keeping with the original language, "be (continually) being filled with the Spirit."

The reason many believers are confused and in doubt as to whether they've been baptized with the Spirit is that they are ignoring the command to be filled with, or controlled by, the Spirit. Only those who are filled observe in their lives the fruit which is the evidence of the Spirit's indwelling presence.

FOUR
THE FULLNESS
OF THE HOLY SPIRIT

The Bible describes the church established by Jesus Christ as a "mystery" (Ephesians 5:32 and elsewhere). It was the secret that God kept concealed from Satan until the time was right to reveal it. But it became a revealed secret after Jesus' resurrection, ascension to the Father, and "return" as "another Comforter," the Holy Spirit.

In Colossians 1:27 the Apostle Paul divulged the very core of God's secret of the church, of true Christianity in the midst of a wicked world. The secret, Paul said simply, is "Christ in you." Yes, Christ living his life in and through the life of the individual believer—purifying, preserving, motivating, and empowering. This is God's design for his church—a body, the body of Christ, composed of individual members each energized and controlled by the living, resurrected Jesus.

To enter into the fullness and fruitfulness of God's secret—Christ in you—you must first of all answer one question. It's very simple. *Do you know Jesus?* Do you really know him? Have you invited him into your life and accepted him as Lord and Savior? Have you yielded your life to him completely, by faith, as best you know how?

If so, then you can answer, "Yes, I know Jesus." But before you can appropriate everything God provides for you in his secret plan for your Christian life, there's another important question you must answer: *Is the Holy Spirit filling you?*

There are three answers you could give to that question. "Yes," "No," or "I'm not sure I know what you mean."

Too many Christians who can say, "Yes, I know Jesus," have to say in answer to this second question, "Just what do you mean, 'Is the Holy Spirit filling me?'"

First, let me tell you what I do *not* mean. I do not mean that you should be having more of the Holy Spirit than you already have. If you've been saved, you have the whole Holy Spirit. He's a person. He doesn't enter into a believer by degrees or stages. Jesus promised, "If any man hear me and open the door, I will come in"—all of him. And that's who the Holy Spirit is—Jesus indwelling the believer by his Spirit. Every Christian has all of God, all of the Spirit in him.

Now, then, what *do* we mean when we talk about being filled with the Spirit? Look at Ephesians 5:18: "And be not drunk with wine, wherein is excess; but be filled with the Spirit."

A COMMAND OF GOD

The first thing we can note about being filled with the Spirit is that God commands it. Paul, in this letter to the Ephesians, is writing under the inspiration of God when he delivers his exhortation to be filled with the Spirit.

Notice, too, that he is talking to all believers. He

doesn't single out the super-saint. Being filled with the Spirit is not optional—it's standard equipment for believers in Christ. It's a sin against God not to be filled.

The command to be Spirit-filled is given in the same breath as the command not to be drunk with wine. Most Christians would be shocked to see a fellow believer staggering into the sanctuary drunk on Sunday morning. But if it's a sin to disobey the command not to be inebriated, isn't it just as much a sin to disobey the command to be filled with the Spirit?

In selecting deacons, some churches put great emphasis on whether or not a man is a tither. But being Spirit-filled should be a much more important qualification. Tithing isn't even explicitly commanded in the New Testament. Being filled with the Spirit is.

It was not without reason that God commanded his people to be filled with his Holy Spirit. Being filled is necessary for:

Purity of Life. The flesh and the Spirit are at war within us. That old flesh is suffering from a terminal illness, but it's not dead and gone yet. You're no better now than before you were saved. The only difference is that now you have the Holy Spirit living in you. If he withdrew himself, you'd be the same as before. God has given you a new nature—Christ in you—but you still have your old nature, too.

And in Galatians 5:19-21, the Bible identifies the works of that old self-nature:

"Adultery, fornication, uncleanness, lasciviousness, idolatry, witchcraft, hatred, variance, emulations, wrath, strife, seditions, heresies, envyings, murders, drunkenness, revelings, and such like."

The Christian has three enemies: the devil, the world, and the flesh; the tempter, the temptation, and the tempted. Two of those forces attack from the outside—the devil and the world. But they can't get in unless sin opens the door. That's where the flesh, the old self-nature, enters the picture. It's the flesh that opens the door and allows the devil and the world to enter and defile the Christian's life and undermine his testimony. Every sin a Christian commits is an inside job.

But if the believer can make the flesh inaccessible to the devil and the world, he can conquer the desires of the flesh. Then he will be protected from the tempter and temptation.

But there's only one way this is possible. "Walk in the Spirit," says Galatians 5:16, "and ye shall not fulfill the lust of the flesh."

Only by walking in the Spirit can we conquer the flesh. Why? Because it's the Holy Spirit who fights and overcomes the flesh. If I try to fight it alone, the flesh overpowers me. The outcome is certain before the first blow is struck.

But it's a fixed fight every time the flesh and the Holy Spirit get in the ring together. I'm the one who determines who will win, because the Spirit of God won't force himself on me. If I insist on trying to defeat flesh with flesh, he won't interfere. But the flesh never really opposes the flesh, of course. That would be a kingdom divided against itself. What actually happens when I fight flesh with flesh is that I forfeit and the flesh wins by default.

But if I ask the Holy Spirit to enter the ring in my place—if I let him take over the fight for me, by giving him control of my life—then he triumphs over the flesh. And when he triumphs, my life no longer exhibits the works of the flesh. Instead, it radiates the fruit of the Spirit.

Picture a tree planted by some water. The tree symbolizes our lives. We all have dead leaves of lust,

sin, and moral decay. How can we get rid of them?
Well, leaves don't just fall off a tree. If it weren't for
the wind and rain, the old leaves would cling to the
branches and still be there the next spring. Then
when the sap began to flow, it would push the old
leaves off, making room for the new.

As Christians, we go around pulling off the dead
leaves. We pluck at this sin and that sin, trying to rip
them from our lives. This doesn't work. We get rid of
the leaves only as we yield to the Holy Spirit. Then
the life-giving sap—his mighty power—surges through
our branches, pushing off the old leaves and bringing
forth the new. To break the power of sin and be pure,
we must focus our attention on Jesus and on his
power, not on our own failures. When we do that, we
don't have to worry. He'll take care of our sin.

Our heavenly Father is the husbandman. He does
the pruning, getting rid of the dead and fruitless
branches. Leave it to him. Let the Spirit of God fill
you and he will purify you.

The filling of the Holy Spirit is also necessary for:

Power in Service. When Elijah stood on Mt. Carmel,
he called the people to him and said, "How long halt
ye between two opinions? if the Lord be God, follow
him: but if Baal, then follow him. And the people
answered him not a word" (1 Kings 18:21).

I've been in that church. Nobody glad. Nobody sad.
Everybody just there, not saying a word.

But remember what happened when the fire fell
from heaven? The people fell on their faces and said,
"The Lord, he is the God; the Lord, he is the God"
vs. 39).

Power for Fruitbearing:
We must be filled with fire from above to
have power for service in the Kingdom of God. How

can you see more people saved? How can you have more baptized? Jesus has given the answer.

In John 15:1 he says, "I am the true vine, and my Father is the husbandman." He goes on to say, "Every branch in me that beareth not fruit he taketh away: and every branch that beareth fruit, he purgeth it, that it may bring forth more fruit." Now look at verse 4: "Abide in me, and I in you. As the branch cannot bear fruit of itself, except it abide in the vine; no more can ye, except ye abide in me."

In verse 5 Jesus summarizes: "I am the vine, ye are the branches. He that abideth in me, and I in him, the same bringeth forth much fruit; for without me ye can do nothing." And in verse 8 he reveals the meaning and purpose of it all—the glorification of the Father: "Herein is my Father glorified, that ye bear much fruit; so shall ye be my disciples."

What is Jesus trying to tell us? That the branch doesn't *produce* fruit—it only *bears* fruit. As a branch, I'm just a fruit rack. The responsibility for fruitfulness is on Jesus. All he asks of us is that we be branches abiding in him, letting his life flow through us.

If you want to bring forth much fruit, then abide much. Some Christians think their lives aren't more fruitful because they need to love the lost more. But the Scripture doesn't tell us how to love the lost. In John 21 Jesus asked Peter three times if Peter loved him. And each time, after Peter said yes, Jesus said, "Feed my sheep." But never once did Jesus ask Peter if he loved sheep! The question was, did he love Jesus?

"If you love me," Jesus said, "feed my sheep."

When the light of this Scripture really dawned on me, I realized that the way to learn to love lost people is to love Jesus!

The most useless preaching I ever did was when I

would exhort people to be soul-winners. I'd say, "You'd better get out and win souls. You ought to be out leading people to Christ." But nobody would go. They lacked the motivation and power to do so. I thank God that he taught me, "Quit trying to make them win souls. Tell them to love me, to let me be Lord, to let the Spirit of God fill their lives. When that's done—when they've enthroned Jesus and appropriated the Holy Spirit—then they will go out and witness and win the lost."

Power for Good Works:
First Corinthians 3:13 says, "Every man's work shall be made manifest . . . what sort it is." The Lord will try our works. Notice, it doesn't say what *size* work we have, but what *sort*. It goes on to reveal that basically there are only two kinds of works. One is made of wood, hay, and stubble, the other of gold, silver, and precious stones.

You see, there are two kinds of good—human good and God's good. There are two kinds of energy—the energy of the flesh and the energy of the Spirit. God rejects human good. To him it's filthy rags. He accepts only the good done in the energy of the Spirit.

God tests our works. He says, "Let's see if you preached, if you taught, if you sang in the Spirit or in the flesh."

A man can live all his life working and doing good, only to stand before Christ and have his entire life of Christian service consumed by the fire of God's judgment—a complete loss. With all that toil and energy you may just be building a bigger haystack.

To stand the test, our work must be done in the power of the Spirit. If a life is lived in the flesh, it's wasted. It will go up in smoke. You'll still be saved, but "as by fire." You'll be like a man awakened in the middle of the night to discover his house is burning. He is able to escape, he is saved, but the house and all his belongings—everything he has worked and saved for—go up in flames.

Be filled with the Spirit. Let him do his work through you. Then your work will be of gold, silver, precious stones—the sort that's acceptable to God because it glorifies him.

A COMMAND TO BE CONTROLLED

God commands every Christian believer to be filled with the Spirit, and it's necessary to obey this command if our lives are to be pure and fruitful.

But there's something else we should understand about this command: It's a command to be *controlled* by the Holy Spirit.

In *The Living Bible,* Ephesians 5:18 reads, " . . . be filled instead with the Holy Spirit, and controlled by him."

To be filled, then, doesn't mean to fill up gradually with the Holy Spirit, like a glass filling with water. You do not grow up in the filling of the Spirit. There's no growing until you are filled. Being filled really means being possessed completely. Remember, the parallel in this verse is drawn from the influence wine exerts over the life of the inebriate. The drunk man doesn't control his own actions. The wine does.

Would you like to be filled with the Spirit? Then there are some questions you need to ask yourself. Do you really want to be controlled by a person who would not tolerate any self-centeredness in your life—a person who would tolerate no envy or jealousy—who would demand that you recognize that you have no rights of your own, that you're a slave—

a person who demands absolute holiness and allows no sin?

That's what it is to be controlled by the Spirit. Two things are involved: The first is:

Deny Self. Realize you're not your own, that you've been bought with a price—the precious blood of Jesus Christ (see 1 Corinthians 6:20).

The testimony of one of my closest friends—now a radiant Spirit-filled preacher of the gospel—may fit the pattern of your life. Saved at the age of nine, he surrendered for the ministry at a very early age. But soon, he says, he discovered that you can be saved and be preaching and teaching good fundamental, conservative doctrine, and yet still have something missing. He says he had no idea what that "something" was, but he would preach victory and live defeat, preach peace and live anxiety, preach love and live a life characterized by criticism, jealousy, envy.

Is that a familiar picture? As a Christian, have you ever felt stale, stagnant, like you had run out of steam? You go to church every time the door is open, hoping that will change you, but it doesn't. There's nothing worse than making yourself go to church. You keep thinking something will happen. You go to "deeper life" conferences, or you read a book and you think that finally you're going to turn a corner, that God's going to lay something on you and change your life completely.

It'll never happen that way. You may have a lot of emotional experiences, you may get inspired, but after two or three weeks you'll fizzle out and hit the valley again. You can talk about the "deeper life" and yet not live it. And that's how it will be until you deny self.

The second thing necessary to a Spirit-controlled life is:

Enthrone Christ. Let Jesus be Lord. Put him in the driver's seat of your life.

You may have come to the point where you said, "There's got to be more to it than this." There is. When you've hit one of those wonderful peaks in your Christian experience, you may have said, "Why can't it always be this way?" It can.

But there's only one way it can. Jesus has got to be Lord of your life.

When Jesus is Lord, there's a change. There's love. You can love people you could never love before. There's joy, a joy you've never known before. There's peace and self-control. And there's victory—over problems, over habits, over sin.

This is what happened in my friend's life. He made Jesus Lord. When you make Jesus Lord, the Holy Spirit fills you.

He is the One who can make the difference—in your life, in your Christian service, in your home.

A COMMAND TO BE CONTINUALLY CONTROLLED

There's another important truth that every believer should understand about being filled with the Holy Spirit: It's not a once-and-for-all experience. In the original language, the verb "be filled" expresses a sense of continuing action that doesn't come through in the English translation. Literally, it says "be being filled."

We are to let the Holy Spirit fill us continually. We are to let him be constantly in control of our lives. We're not to live a roller coaster existence—up one minute and down the next, on a mountaintop today

and in the valley of despair tomorrow. We're not to
live from one little inspiration, one little holy kick to
the next, falling into defeat and discouragement in
between. Our lives should be a daily walk, a constant
abiding, a state of continually being filled with the
Spirit.

For that reason, the question you ask yourself
should not be, "Has the Holy Spirit filled me?" It
should be, "Is the Holy Spirit at this moment filling
me? Is he right now exercising complete control over
my life?"

Is he? There are three ways you can be sure. The
first is:

Instant Confession of Sin. The very moment you
become aware of having sinned, confess that sin to
God, accept his forgiveness, and commit yourself to
rely on his power to keep you from doing that sin
again. Unconfessed sin is the great divider. It's like
an obstruction blocking the flow of life-giving sap
from the vine into the branch. Power is stifled. The
fruit crop is aborted. The only way to remove this
destructive obstacle of sin is through confession.
Instant confession brings instant forgiveness. It
immediately restores power and fruitbearing poten-
tial.

Another way to be sure that we're being
continually filled and controlled by the Holy Spirit is
by:

Immediate Obedience. The moment the Spirit of God
impresses you to speak, to witness, to pray, or
whatever his instructions might be, your response
must be to obey immediately. Jesus said that from
the lives of those believing in him would flow "rivers
of living water" (John 7:38). But God can't continually

pour himself into us when we're shutting off the flow through disobedience. And it is a continual filling of the Holy Spirit God wants to give us (vs. 39).

Is the Holy Spirit filling you right now? Is he in absolute, sovereign control over you?

Not if you have any unconfessed sin in your life. Not if he is directing you to make some decision, to take some specific course in life, and you are hesitating or refusing to obey.

But let me warn you. There's no magic formula to being continually filled with the Holy Spirit. It can't be made to happen just by saying certain words. It happens when there is a full commitment of your mind, soul, and body to Jesus. The Holy Spirit wants to control every facet of your life. When you come to the place where you want what the Holy Spirit wants, he fills you—and keeps filling you.

If you want the Holy Spirit to fill you, pray for God to do a work of conviction in you. Ask him to show you the areas of sin and disobedience in your life. A reconciliation, a restitution is needed to clear the way for the filling you desire.

Call on the Lord to reveal your true self to you, so that you can deny that self and recognize Jesus as absolute Lord. Then, not looking for a feeling or an experience, but simply by faith, appropriate the filling of the Holy Spirit, and thank the Lord for granting it as Jesus becomes truly Lord of all.

To seal your assurance that you're being constantly filled and controlled by the Holy Spirit, one more thing is required:

Constant Trusting. That which must follow instant confession and immediate obedience, if you are to be continually filled, is best described with the word Jesus used: "abiding." Now that we've confessed, we must continually confess. Now that we've obeyed, we must keep on obeying. Now that we've trusted, we must continually trust.

We must trust that the Holy Spirit is fulfilling the promises made to those who want to be filled—the promise that he is present with us, the promise that he is working in us, and the promise that he is working through us. These things we must know by faith, whether or not we see spectacular evidence to confirm them.

This is abiding. To abide is to be continually filled and constantly walking in the center of God's will.

FIVE
THE FRUIT OF THE SPIRIT

If you have sincerely and without reservation yielded control of your life to the Holy Spirit; if you are instantly confessing each sin that comes to your awareness; if you are giving immediate obedience to every command of God; if you are abiding in unshakable faith, confident that the Holy Spirit is fulfilling his promises—if all these conditions prevail, then you be sure you are continually being filled with the Holy Spirit.

God wants you to know beyond the shadow of a doubt that you are being filled. He doesn't want you searching for mystical experiences to prove it. He doesn't expect you to wait or work for miraculous manifestations of his power and presence. Through his written Word, he has pointed out the evidence that signifies his fullness in the life of the believer.

And the evidence is moral, not miraculous!

THE FRUIT OF THE SPIRIT:
A PRODUCT OF FULLNESS

In Galatians 5:16 (NASB), God reveals the test of whether we're controlled by the Holy Spirit: "But I say, walk by the Spirit, and you will not carry out the desire of the flesh."

How can you know the will of God? How often I've heard that question! It's not your responsibility to find the will of God. It's his responsibility to reveal it to you. Your responsibility is to be willing to do it, to obey the instructions of the Holy Spirit.

By nature, we don't want to obey the Holy Spirit. In ourselves we want to do just the opposite of what the Spirit wants. But when we're possessed and controlled by the Spirit, we don't have to force ourselves to obey God's law. Obedience is a natural response of the Spirit-filled person, because he is controlled not by his own nature but by the nature of the Spirit. You don't have to work at it. You don't have to fight for it. The Holy Spirit does it for you!

The Works of the Flesh. When you follow your old human nature, you do the "wrong things" it wants you to do. They come almost in the order in which they are listed in the Scriptures, beginning with verse 19 of Galatians 5: "Impure thoughts, eagerness for lustful pleasure, idolatry, spiritism (that is, encouraging the activity of demons), hatred and fighting, jealousy and anger, constant effort to get the best for yourself, complaints and criticisms, the feeling that everyone else is wrong except those in your own little group—and there will be wrong doctrine, envy, murder, drunkenness, wild parties, and all that sort of thing" (TLB).

"Impure thoughts." The thought always precedes

the action. If your thoughts are not purified by that renewing of your mind that comes with being filled by the Spirit, you will think impure thoughts—and impure actions will follow.

"Idolatry." We think of idolatry in terms of images carved out of wood or stone. But anything that stands between you and Jesus, preventing you from doing his will, is an idol. It can be business, sports, a hobby, a person. It can be your family or your wife. You may have married someone *you* wanted to marry, not someone the Lord led you to marry, and that person may now be the idol that draws your allegiance away from the Lord Jesus.

"Jealousy." Jealousy is a venom that poisons the lifeblood of the church. One Christian sees another filled with the Spirit and bearing fruit for the Lord, and he becomes jealous. He may try to imitate the other believer's spirituality, or he may try to cripple him with criticism or to undermine his work. If only such Christians would realize that such power is available to any born-again believer who will yield to the complete control of the Spirit. But that power is available, not to be used by the Christian, but to make use of the Christian.

If you're not filled with the Holy Spirit, there will be a "constant effort to get the best for yourself." A lot of Christians are always down in the mouth. They're gloomy, discouraged, pessimistic. In most cases it's because things aren't going quite the way they want them to. They aren't getting the best, or what they think is best, for themselves. There's no cheering up such a down-in-the-dumps Christian. The desires of the self-nature are insatiable. Nothing is ever good enough or perfect enough to suit the self. For the self-seeking, self-pitying Christian there's only one remedy—full surrender to the Holy Spirit.

In the unfilled Christian there will also be "the feeling that everyone else is wrong except those in your own litle group," and there will be "wrong doctrine." Many who think they're so right are going to find out they're so wrong. This can happen in a denomination, a church, a prayer group. It can happen any place where people who are not filled with the Spirit gather together.

Those are the works of the flesh. Not very desirable products, are they? And yet they are all too evident in many Christian lives, because believers refuse to heed the Spirit.

But listen carefully now: A person doesn't have to be doing all of these "wrong things" to know that he is being controlled by his own evil self-nature and not by the Holy Spirit. If just one of these things has got you, it's evidence that you're not filled. For you couldn't be doing that thing if God had complete control of your life, if you were totally possessed by the Holy Spirit.

What's Inside Comes Out. How can you know whether you're being continually filled with the Holy Spirit? If you really want to find out what's inside that old vessel of yours, just notice what comes out when it's broken! If it's full of mud, when you break it mud comes out.

What oozes forth when things go wrong, when somebody rubs you the wrong way, when you're in a hurry and the car ahead of you won't move over and let you pass? (I sometimes think we could be pretty good Christians if we didn't have to drive!) But seriously, if there's one dirty thing in the vial, that will be the first thing to gush into the open when you're broken. When your coating of cultural refinement and conventional courtesy crumbles, the real you will be exposed.

The Fruit of the Spirit. The problem is, though, we don't want to talk about sin. Nobody wants to just come clean and say, "I'm dirty." And yet we must if we want to grow. It's a tremendous thing to let Jesus show us what we are like inside, apart from his Holy Spirit. It's dirty in there, in that old self-nature. Nobody has anything to boast about. This must be acknowledged, so the old flesh can be vanquished. Then, and only then, can the Holy Spirit control us.

But when you do give the Holy Spirit full control, he produces an entirely different crop of fruit from that produced by the flesh. He brings forth the fruit of the Spirit. Notice, it's singular—"fruit." It has many aspects, but it's just one fruit. As the Holy Spirit drives out every trace of fleshly fruit when he controls a life, he also brings forth every aspect of his spiritual fruit in the life he controls.

When you are filled with the Holy Spirit, your life will abound in all elements of spiritual fruit—and only when you are filled. It's possible for some people naturally to possess what appear to be some aspects of spiritual fruit in their lives. But a complete and abundant display of the fruit of the Spirit is a product of being filled with the Spirit. It comes about in no other way.

And here is the fruit of the Spirit, as it's described in Galatians 5:22, 23 (NASB).

"Love." Love for him, for Jesus. "Waves of liquid love," Charles Finney once said in describing the wonderful capacity for the love that swept over him when he was filled with the Spirit.

I remember how love saturated my life when I first began to experience the power of the Holy Spirit in my life. I overflowed with love for Jesus. I used to fly over Dallas, returning from preaching a revival in some other part of the country, and when I would see lights below I'd say, "There's a home; I wonder if those people are saved." "There's a family. Are they saved?" Life was a constant adventure. I found it easy to stop people on the street or in a restaurant to tell them about Jesus. I would go anywhere to preach his message.

When you're filled with the Spirit, you're filled with love.

"Joy." Every day, for the Spirit-filled Christian, is a joyful experience. Now notice, I didn't say that every experience would be a happy one. Happiness depends on happenings. When good things happen, we're happy; when bad things happen, we're not.

But joy is an attitude emanating from the Spirit of God. With the joy he gives us, we don't have to live under the circumstances. We can live above them. Joy flows from our knowledge of his promises and our confidence in his ability to fulfill those promises. And joy continues to flow, even when circumstances are bad, because we know that "all things work together for good to them that love God."

"Peace." Peace presupposes that there has been a battle and that the battle has been fought to a clear-cut conclusion. One side has won, the other side has lost. That's what happens when you yield your life completely to the control of the Holy Spirit. You've stopped fighting and stepped aside. The Holy Spirit has stepped in and utterly destroyed the enemy, casting out Satan and conquering your old nature.

The best you could ever manage in your own power was an armed truce. More than likely, it was a perpetual struggle in which you were always down and sometimes out. But when the Holy Spirit fills you, the battle has been fought, the victory won, and you have a peace such as you've never known—a peace that passes all human understanding.

"Patience." This is the one that's the hardest to

counterfeit. You can pretend to love, to be joyful, to be at peace with yourself, God, and your fellowman. But if you're impatient, everybody knows it. It'll show. It's the telltale sign that you're not being filled with the Holy Spirit.

With the Spirit in control, there's no hurry. You can wait. Do you know why? Because you're on the wave-length of eternity. You've stepped into the mainstream of everlasting life. And when you have forever, you can take a few moments out to play with your children, to listen to that friend who wants to tell about some pleasant—or unpleasant—experience, to comfort that sick person, to tell that wretched, sinful, undeserving lost person about Christ. But without the Holy Spirit in control, you're one of the "now generation." You want things your way immediately, if not sooner, because your old nature is impatient. The Holy Spirit alone produces patience.

"Kindness." Here we have the handmaiden of patience. Kindness is the quality that shows outwardly when you are a patient person inwardly. Some people seem naturally kind; others work at it and learn to be kind. But such cultivated kindness— kindness that does not flow from Spirit-given patience—sooner or later reverts to its true temperament. Given enough stress, it will crack. Kindness with its roots in the patience of the Holy Spirit goes on being kind, even when the object of the kindness becomes loathsome, ungrateful, or impudent.

"Goodness." There are some naturally "good" people, too, and what a tragedy that can be! Until the Holy Spirit fills you, you are good for nothing but sin. "Good" lost people can burn in hell while those still living talk about what good people they were. It's a sin for a "good" Christian not to be filled with the Holy Spirit. Jesus said, "There is one good, and that is God." Real goodness is God-likeness.

"Faithfulness." In the King James version this word is rendered "faith," but it should be "faithfulness." Usually we think of this as denoting faith, or faithfulness toward God. But it's more than that. It's a quality that should permeate every relationship of our lives. Faithfulness toward your families. Faithfulness toward your friends. Faithfulness toward your employer if you're a jobholder. Faithfulness toward your employees if you have people working for you. Faithfulness toward your church, your community, mankind.

It involves dependability. It means being where you said you would be when you said you would be there. It means doing what you said you would do. You have a duty to the world—the duty to bear faithful witness to Christ and his salvation. But that witness rings hollow unless we are faithful in all things. That kind of faithfulness comes only from God.

"Gentleness." Do you know what a gentle horse is? It's a trained, disciplined animal that has submitted to the control of a master in whom it has unquestioning confidence. That's the picture of the Spirit-filled Christian. If you're filled, you'll be gentle. You won't be jumpy, kicking back at every little annoyance. You won't stampede away in your own direction when something doesn't suit you. You'll wait patiently to obey the slightest pressure from the Master's reins. You will be willing to submit to God's control. Being "meek" or gentle may also be defined as being "teachable."

"Self-control." Actually, this means "self-under-control." It means God in control of you. You can't control self, so let God control you. This is the very essence of being continually filled with the Spirit.

THE FRUIT OF THE SPIRIT:
A PROJECTION OF CHARACTER

If you are being continually filled and controlled by the Spirit you will, as I said before, show forth all of these aspects of the fruit of the Spirit. The reason is quite simple, and I'm sure you've already discovered it: You'll possess all aspects of the fruit of the Spirit because the fruit of the Spirit is really the projection of God's character through your life.

Christ in You. Jesus said: "The one who obeys me is the one who loves me; and because he loves me, my father will love him; and I will too, and I will reveal myself to him" (John 14:21, TLB). He will also reveal himself *through* you.

The Holy Spirit is best described as "the other Jesus," or the Spirit of Jesus—his personality in you. When you are filled with the Holy Spirit, the fullness of Jesus—his life and power and character—dwells in you and flows through you in everything you do and say.

The fruit of the Spirit is a product of the filling of the Spirit, because the fruit in reality is the projection of the character of the Spirit—the character of Christ in you, the hope of glory.

And if you're continually being filled with the Holy Spirit, you will do the works that Jesus did when he walked this earth in a human body. And greater works than these will you do, as he promised in John 14:12, because he works through you to spread his love, joy, peace, patience, goodness, kindness, faithfulness, gentleness, and self-control.

In the last week you may have walked by hundreds of people without ever thinking of witnessing to them about Jesus. The student at the next desk in school. The janitor. The guy who works with you at the office. The man who put gas in your car. The woman who waited on you in the department store. Your next-door neighbor.

But let me tell you, if you're filled with the Spirit you won't walk past people without wanting to tell them about Jesus! Talking about the one you love is as natural as breathing.

The Promise Is to You! Don't you want to be filled with the Holy Spirit? Don't you want to experience all of the life-giving fullness of Christ in your life?

Speaking of the outpouring of the Holy Spirit into the hearts of believers, Peter said in Acts 2:39 that "the promise is unto you."

If you really want to be filled, you can be—today, right now! You can claim the wonderful promises given you by the Lord himself. Remember those precious words spoken by Jesus: "Blessed are they which do hunger and thirst after righteousness: for they shall be filled."

SIX
THE GIFTS OF
THE HOLY SPIRIT

Before we begin to look into the subject of spiritual gifts, a topic of tremendous importance to today's church, there are two things we must get clear in our minds. One is the fact that there's a difference between "gifts of the Spirit" and "the gift of the Spirit."

"The gift of the Spirit" is what we have talked about already. It is the Holy Spirit himself. This is set forth plainly in Acts 2:38 and reaffirmed in Galatians 4:6, Romans 5:5, and innumerable other verses in the Scriptures. The gift of the Spirit, the Spirit himself, is given to all believers, as we are told in Acts 2:39. And, you might say, he is God's birthday gift to us, for he is given at the time of spiritual birth. Remember how, in Acts 19:1-4, Paul asked a group of John the Baptist's disciples, thinking they were Christians, if they had not received the Holy Spirit "when you believed." Finally, in Romans 8:9 we are told that unless we have received this gift, the gift of the Holy Spirit himself, we are "none of his"; that is, we're not Christians at all.

The other thing we need to understand is that there's a difference between the "gifts of the Spirit" and "the fruit of the Spirit." Gifts pertain to service, and not primarily to character. Fruit pertains to quality of life and has everything to do with character. It's possible for an unspiritual, carnal Christian to exercise gifts of the Spirit, sometimes with remarkable results. But it's not possible for an unspiritual, un-Spirit-filled Christian to display the fruit of the Spirit.

This is a frequent source of confusion to many Christians. Here is a preacher delivering a powerful, magnificent message, resulting in people being saved by the scores. Yet there's sin in his life; he isn't a Spirit-filled Christian; his life doesn't display the fruit of the Spirit—love, joy, peace, long-suffering, gentleness, goodness, faithfulness, meekness, and Spirit-control. What's the answer? He is exercising a gift of the Holy Spirit in serving the Lord, even though he is quenching the fruit of the Holy Spirit by not yielding his life to the Spirit's control.

With these things in mind—that "the gift of the Spirit," "the gifts of the Spirit," and "the fruit of the Spirit" are all different things—let's examine the great truth regarding the *gifts* of the Spirit.

THEIR SOURCE AND PURPOSE

Where do "gifts of the Spirit" come from? The answer is in the question itself. "Of the Spirit" means "from the Spirit." They come from the Spirit himself. The *New American Standard Bible* states this with sparkling clarity. In this translation 1 Corinthians 12:1 reads: "Now, concerning spiritual gifts, brethren, I do not want you to be unaware." Verses 9, 11 identify the source of the gifts—"the one Spirit."

The Living Bible calls spiritual gifts "special abilities," extraordinary abilities that mere human beings cannot have. This is an important clue to God's purpose in giving spiritual gifts. He intends for his church to be spiritual and supernatural in its operations, just as it is spiritual and supernatural in its origin.

Jesus told the original disciples, "I will not leave you comfortless." Jesus had just told them that he would be leaving them, and the disciples were deeply concerned. They had reason to be. As mysterious and confusing as things had been for them with the Lord among them, what would it be like with him gone? But Jesus would not leave them comfortless, as abandoned orphans in the world. He would fill the void. He would send "another Comforter," someone like himself, and it would be just as if he were still here. The Comforter, the Holy Spirit, would do in the believer just what Jesus would have done if he were still here in the flesh.

God's Provision. One of the big problems in the church today is that we believe the church to be supernatural in its origin, but not in its operations. When we experience a loss of power and effectiveness, it drives us to rely on human resources, the energy of the flesh, in an effort to correct the problem. When the power of the early church isn't evident in our churches, we have to save face, so we bring the teachings of God down to the level of our experience. We're satisfied with believing that Jesus never intended us to have supernatural power in daily living. We delude ourselves with the false doctrine that once we become mature and capable in our human abilities, this will substitute for the supernatural power of old.

Where did we get this idea that we're not to expect

the supernatural in our Christian service? Certainly not from Jesus. He said, "He that believeth on me, the works that I do shall he do also; and greater works than these shall he do" (John 14:12). If we're not doing greater works than Jesus did when he was here in the flesh, we're not living up to what he intended for us.

Our Example. In Jesus' life on earth, we have the pattern for fulfilling his intention that we should experience supernatural power and ability in our lives. Jesus depended absolutely on the Father. He said, "The Son can do nothing of himself" (John 5:19), and, "I can of mine own self do nothing" (John 5:30).

Jesus refused to rely on his own inherent divine power, choosing rather to depend totally on the Father. For example, he could have turned the stones into bread. There's nothing wrong with eating, you know. Jesus was hungry after forty days and nights of fasting in the wilderness. He could have reasoned, "The Father gave me the kind of body that must have food; he gave me this appetite; so surely he expects me to provide food for it." But in order to rely completely on the Father, he refused to use his own power. He went hungry.

Jesus says, "As my Father hath sent me, even so send I you" (John 20:21). In other words, "I send you into the world with the same resources and the same instructions as my Father gave me when he sent me into the world, and you are to do just as I have done."

So the church is to live in absolute dependence on the Father, just as Jesus did. How? By refusing to rely on human resources—by relying 100 percent on God. Now, I'm not saying not to use human resources at all—I'm talking about relying on ourselves for spiritual results.

Jesus says, "As my Father hath sent me, even so send I you" (John 20:21). In other words, "I send you into the world with the same resources and the same instructions as my Father gave me when he sent me into the world, and you are to do just as I have done."

So the church is to live in absolute dependence on the Father, just as Jesus did. How? By refusing to rely on human resources—by relying 100 percent on God. Now, I'm not saying not to use human resources at all—I'm talking about relying on ourselves for spiritual results.

I'm tired of everything being predictable because it has all been planned and programmed down to the last note of the invitational hymn. And if something happens that we didn't plan and program, we're suspicious of it. The truth is, if it's not supernatural it's superficial. If we can explain it in human terms, that's the time when we really ought to be suspicious of it, because that means it's the result of human effort and not the power of God working through us as he intended.

Influence or Power? We often confuse influence with power. The two are not synonymous. We think that with our big churches we can prevail on the powers that be in our society and really get things done. Well, the New Testament church didn't have much influence. It couldn't even keep Peter out of jail—but it had power enough to pray him out! Daniel didn't have enough influence to stay out of the den of lions, but God had the power to get him out.

God's will is that his church should be supernatural in its operations. The provision he has made for this supernatural performance is his Holy Spirit, who gives to each believer special gifts to be used in his service.

SPIRITUAL BIRTHDAY GIFTS

The gift of the Holy Spirit and the gifts of the Holy Spirit are "birthday gifts," given at the time of salvation. Every believer has at least one of these gifts of special, supernatural ability. We're told this not only in 1 Corinthians 12:1, but also in Romans 12:5, 6: "So we, being many, are one body in Christ, and every one members one of another. Having then gifts differing according to the grace that is given to us . . ." Ephesians 4:8 says: "When he ascended up on high, he led captivity captive, and gave gifts unto men." The gifts of the Spirit are the spoils of war, the spoils of victory. In his death and resurrection, Jesus completely demolished Satan's dominion and power once and for all. He took the spoils of power in this world, and now he shares them with all Christians.

Many Christians find it hard to believe that they have a gift. You may not recognize your gift, but that doesn't mean you don't have one. According to God's Word, every Christian has at least one, and has had it since the moment of salvation.

Given to Be Used. It's important to realize, too, that you are expected to recognize your gift and let God use it. In 1 Peter 4:10 God commands us, "As every man hath received the gift, even so minister the same one to another, as good stewards of the manifold grace of God." It's as much a sin to disobey that commandment as any other. It's a sin not to use the gifts of the Spirit. If I don't use my gifts, I've buried the talent God gave me and there will be an accounting at the judgment-seat of Christ.

What a shame that so many spiritual gifts are lost to Christ and the church because those who possess them don't know they have them, or else know but simply don't put them to work.

Gifts—Not Rewards. There's another thing we should understand about the gifts of the Holy Spirit: they are not rewards for spirituality. They are given without regard for degree of commitment. This is understandable, since they are given at the moment of salvation. When a child is born physically, the natural abilities given to him are in no way related to the kind of character he will have later in life. Likewise, spiritual gifts have nothing to do with how spiritual a person is. They do not give positive proof of fullness of the Spirit.

Paul commended the Corinthians on their spiritual gifts, saying that "ye come behind in no gift" (1 Corinthians 1:7). And he certainly wasn't exaggerating. In that church they had every gift, and they were exercising them all with vigor. Yet in 3:3 of his letter Paul chided them for being so unspiritual: "Ye are yet carnal . . . and walk as men," that is, as lost people. Immorality, strife, and division ran rampant among them. And yet they were exercising spiritual gifts, one of them—the gift of tongues—to the point that it had become a serious problem.

But let me reemphasize that a gift is not a sign of spirituality. A man can preach and multitudes hear him and be saved. That's a gift. It doesn't mean the man is Spirit-filled. And a gift is a gift, presented at spiritual birth. It can't be received through any amount of praying, weeping, waiting, or working.

Gifts That Differ. Some say there is one spiritual gift that everybody should have—the gift of tongues. This idea did not come from the Scriptures. I don't mean to offend anyone, and I know there are many sincere Christians who hold to this doctrine. But I must repeat: It simply is not scriptural.

What do the Scriptures say? We've already read

Romans 12:6, which refers to "gifts differing." Now
let's look at 1 Corinthians 12:4-10. Notice that this
passage begins with the statement that there are
"diversities"—that is, differences—of gifts. The same
thought is repeated in verse 6. In verse 8, Paul begins
to name various gifts, saying "to one" is given such
and such a gift, "to another" a different gift, and "to
another" still another gift. In verse 10, Paul concludes
by saying "to another"—notice, not to all—"divers
kinds of tongues; to another"—again, not to all—"the
interpretation of tongues."

Spirit-Assigned Gifts. The gifts of the Spirit differ
from one individual to another. And the Spirit
decides who shall have what gift: "But all these
worketh that one and the selfsame Spirit, dividing to
every man severally as he will" (vs. 11).

The Spirit passes out the different gifts to different
people according to his will. If we insist that
everybody must have the same gift, it leads to two
things, both bad. It leads to defeat and frustration for
a lot of earnest but misguided believers, and it can
lead to a false experience from the devil. If you
stubbornly demand an experience God doesn't want
you to have, you're liable to get an experience that is
not from God, but from Satan.

What we need to be concerned about is whether
we've made ourselves completely available to God—
not whether he has made available to us some gift or
experience we think we should have. Besides, if we
all had the same gift, the church would be a
monstrosity. What if every part of our body wanted
to be an eye? We couldn't smell, feel, walk, eat, or
work. All we could do would be to see. (Read
1 Corinthians 12:14-27 in this regard.)

In creating the body of Christ, his church, God
hasn't built a monstrosity. He has built an organism

with different members, having different functions
that harmonize and complement each other. Men do
not decide who shall have such gifts. The gifts are
sovereignly bestowed by the Spirit himself. In
Hebrews 2:4, this truth is plainly stated again: "God
also bearing them witness, both with signs and
wonders, and with divers miracles, and gifts of the
Holy Ghost, according to his own will."

Since the Holy Spirit decides who gets which gifts,
there certainly should be no envy or coveting among
Christians with regard to spiritual gifts, although we
do have the phrase "covet earnestly the best gifts"
(1 Corinthians 12:31). But which gifts are the best or
most important? The gifts best for you may not be
best for me. Each of us needs to seek those particular
gifts most suited to us, and those are the gifts which
the Spirit has chosen for us anyway. He knows best!

Paul goes on to say, "I show unto you a more
excellent way." In other words, there is a way that is
much better than coveting one another's gifts and
quarreling over whose gift is the most important. In
the next chapter, 1 Corinthians 13, Paul describes
that more excellent way—the way of love.

KEYS TO POWER

Another point must be emphasized concerning
spiritual gifts: they do not refer to natural ability or
talent. Natural ability doesn't qualify you for work in
the church. The only thing that qualifies you for
Christian service is the operation of the Holy Spirit
in your life.

There was a time when I thought that if a church
could line up enough schoolteachers to teach Sunday
school, it would be on the road to fantastic growth.
But I came to realize that some schoolteachers are the
worst Sunday school teachers. (Notice, I said

"some.") It all depends on whether or not they possess the spiritual gifts for teaching the Word of God. A Christian can be a wonderful schoolteacher—and let me say here that this, itself, can be a spiritual gift—but without the gift for teaching God's Word, he or she will get only human results at best in teaching a Sunday school class.

The reason so many churches are just struggling along, never experiencing anything particularly exciting, is that they have ignored what the Bible says about the gift of teaching. They have people in teaching positions who do not have the Spirit's gift for teaching.

You Do and You Can. The Spirit's gifts are supernatural abilities. They produce results that can't be explained in terms of human resources. And every believer has at least one such gift.

If you're a Christian and you know that you have trusted Christ and received spiritual birth, quit saying there is nothing you can do. You can do something, and you are commanded by the Word of God to do it. When people begin to recognize their supernatural abilities and exercise their gifts with a continual filling of the Holy Spirit, then the church will be supernatural in its operation—and not until.

Humility is the crying need among Christians today. By humility, I don't mean punishing yourself or the false modesty of those who keep saying, "I can't do anything." I mean simply not seeing yourself as being Number One. The Christian should expect the supernatural in his ministry. You should forget the idea that your work depends on *your* ability, training, and preparation. Instead, rely completely on the gift—or really, the Giver.

And if you have a certain gift, you know better how to exercise that supernatural ability than anyone else. You shouldn't let anyone distract you with human advice or even with misapplied scriptural exhortations.

Rely on the Spirit. But above all, you must not let self stand in the way, with its puny ineffectual talents and abilities. Rely on the Spirit. If you make mistakes, God will work it out, because you're yielded to doing his will.

Today we're inclined to depend on gimmicks and man-made devices to get things done. It's worthwhile to remember that at Pentecost 120 people had the rapt attention of all the hundreds of thousands of people who had gathered in Jerusalem to observe a holy day. They didn't have TV, billboards, newspaper ads, or advance press releases on what was about to happen. All they had was the Holy Spirit, the gifts with which he had endued them, and the magnetic attracting power of God.

KEYS TO SERVICE

The gifts of the Holy Spirit are gifts for service. They may, and do, bless the individuals who possess them, but that isn't their primary purpose. They are given primarily to profit everyone in the fellowship of the church. As 1 Corinthians 12:7 states, the manifestation of the Spirit through the different gifts "is given to every man to profit withal," or "for the common good" (NASB). Or take Ephesians 4:11, which says the various gifts were given "for the perfecting of the saints [all Christians], for the work of the ministry, for the edifying of the body of Christ." Spiritual gifts are to profit the entire body, not merely to provide personal glory or enjoyment.

In Acts we see the gift of tongues as evidence of the Spirit's presence and as having the effect of facilitating the spread of the gospel. In 1 Corinthians, we read that it was given for edification of the believer when used in public, but was not to be used in this manner except with the presence of another person possessing the gift of interpretation of tongues. In private, a believer could exercise the gift of tongues to edify himself. Not to glorify himself, but to edify himself—that is, to be strengthened spiritually.

This is the Spirit-inspired Word of God concerning the use of this gift, and the Spirit will never lead anyone individually to do anything contrary to his written Word.

Furthermore, since all gifts are sovereignly given, according to the will of God, nobody has to tell you how to get any particular gift—and that includes the gift of tongues. If God means for you to have this gift, you will have it. Trying to get it will only cause problems.

Abuse of this gift of tongues is a weapon used by the devil to counteract the genuine movement of God. It has been known to split churches that were on fire for the Lord, to wreck revivals that were sweeping whole nations. But Christians needn't let Satan get away with tricks such as this. All they need to do is consult the Word of God and do as it says. Then all gifts will be used as God intended them to be.

DISCOVERY POSSIBLE

One last thing concerning spiritual gifts—they can be recognized. God intends these gifts to be used, so why would he try to hide them from us? In recognizing our gifts, we should look for two things:

Personal Inclination. The Spirit often leads us to discover a spiritual gift by giving us a desire to involve ourselves in the type of service to which the gift is related. Here we must be careful, however. Wants and desires can be implanted from other sources—Satan, self, a Christian friend, a parent. In determining what our gifts are, we need more than personal interests as a guide.

Public Recognition. A second factor to look for is recognition by other Spirit-led people. If an ability is a gift of the Spirit, and not just natural talent, the church will recognize it and use it, and God will bless it.

A good friend of mine tells about his experience in discovering his spiritual gift. Because he could speak with eloquence and because he had a strong personal inclination to be an evangelist, he decided that his gift was that of evangelism. But he got few calls from churches to come and lead evangelistic services. When he did get an evangelistic meeting, people, to put it mildly, weren't saved by the multitudes. Finally it occurred to him, "Maybe my gift isn't evangelism, after all." And he was right. He became a pastor. One of the most dynamic churches in the state of Texas extended a call to him. He accepted, and now God is adding to the church daily in power and in numbers, as people are being saved and Christians are growing in grace and in personal fellowship with the Lord.

As an evangelist, he had the inclination and the natural ability. But the church didn't use it, and God didn't bless it. As a pastor, the church is using his gift and God is blessing it with supernatural results.

IS YOUR GIFT BEING USED?

Do you know what your gift is? Are you letting God use it? If not, ask God to reveal to you your gifts. The church has been too long without the use of the gifts of too many born-again believers. Don't deny the body of Christ the benefit of your spiritual gift. And don't deny yourself the joy and blessing of knowing that God is able to use you in the way that he intended when he called you unto himself through Jesus Christ.

Discover your gift, rely on the Holy Spirit, and your life will produce supernatural results for the Lord Jesus.

The next section of this book is designed to help you make this exciting discovery.

SEVEN
DISCOVERING
YOUR SPIRITUAL GIFT

When you were born physically, you had certain natural abilities. They were part of your physical nature. If you have been born again, receiving the spiritual new birth by accepting Jesus Christ as your Savior, you now have certain spiritual abilities. These new spiritual abilities are part of your spiritual nature. They are gifts from God, brought into your life by the Holy Spirit. You can't "work them up" on your own and you can't imitate them, because no one has a spiritual gift unless God has given that gift to him.

And no child of God, according to the Scriptures, has been left out. Everyone has at least one gift. "Unto every one of us is given grace according to the measure of the gift of Christ" (Ephesians 4:7).

God's purpose in giving us spiritual gifts, the Bible says, is twofold: (1) For our own spiritual development and fulfillment; (2) For the welfare and building up of the body of Christ, the church. (See Romans 12:3-5; 1 Corinthians 12:1-31; Ephesians 4:7-16.)

The Bible emphasizes that these special abilities are to be used to produce Christlikeness in the individual Christian and to equip him to build up the body of Christ, the church, both in numbers and strength. The gifts were designed to benefit the body of Christ by promoting unity, maturity, and growth.

The early church stressed the importance of spiritual gifts. Unfortunately this emphasis faded in the church of later years, having seen some signs of revival only recently.

Undeniable, however, the truths pertaining to the gifts of the Spirit are among the most important in the Scriptures to the Christian who would live an abundant, fruitful life in today's world. They are invaluable. Understanding these truths and discovering and developing our gifts, with the guidance and power of the Holy Spirit, are vital necessities to fulfilling our individual roles in the body of Christ. In no other way can the church fulfill its role in the world.

SPIRITUAL ROBBERY

At the moment three shortcomings common among Christians are robbing individual believers and the church of much of the benefit they could be deriving from spiritual gifts.

First, most spiritual gifts are being neglected. Christians either refuse to believe they possess such gifts, or else through ignorance or neglect fail to exercise their gifts properly. What a waste! God has poured out special abilities on every one of us, and most of these special abilities never are put to work, either for our joy or for our Savior's glory.

Second, misunderstandings about gifts are causing friction and disharmony in the church. Christians who fail to recognize and understand the gifts of others are reacting with jealousy or indifference (or even suspicion) to evidence of the gifts. This is resulting in reduced effectiveness of many gifts and discouragement of those who possess them.

Third, some who know they possess certain gifts are, because they don't fully understand the nature and purpose of such gifts, inclined to belittle others who don't show evidence of the same gifts. This, too, is leading to division and ineffectiveness.

The insights that follow, gleaned from the studies of many Bible scholars, are designed to aid you in understanding and identifying spiritual gifts, and discovering the gifts that you personally have been given by the Spirit. Enter this study prayerfully and expectantly. Gaining the ability to recognize spiritual gifts in others, and determining your own gift, could be the most exciting and rewarding experience you have had since accepting Jesus Christ as your Lord and Savior.

SOME FACTS ABOUT GIFTS

Two things need to be understood concerning the nature of spiritual gifts. First, they are special abilities—not offices, not ministries, not fruits. They are abilities to do certain things, and therefore they are concerned with service. They enable the Christian to do things nonbelievers can't do, things even the Christian couldn't do before becoming a Christian and receiving the gifts. Second, spiritual gifts and what we commonly call talents are two different things. Talents are natural abilities or developed skills. Spiritual gifts are spiritual abilities, abilities directed and energized by the Holy Spirit. Talents produce natural results. Spiritual gifts produce supernatural results. Talents may be used in the exercise of spiritual gifts, but often spiritual gifts are exercised in spite of, or in the absence of, natural talents. Even if natural talents are involved, the results still are supernatural. That is, they are beyond explanation in terms of human ability alone.

Spiritual gifts also are varied and numerous. Many are mentioned specifically in various Bible passages such as Romans 12, 1 Corinthians 12, and Ephesians 4.

CATEGORIES OF SPIRITUAL GIFTS

The Scriptures divide spiritual gifts into readily identifiable categories or groupings. The three major divisions are:

Motivations (Romans 12:3-8; 1 Corinthians 12:4).

Ministries (1 Corinthians 12:5, 27, 28; Ephesians 4:11, 12).

Manifestations (1 Corinthians 12:6, 7).

Let me pause here to note that Bible scholars view the subject of spiritual gifts in a number of different ways, and some would disagree with the categories I have just listed. After attending an advanced seminar on spiritual gifts and making a long, careful independent study of the Bible passages pertaining to gifts, I became convinced that dividing the gifts into these categories enables us to understand them better. It also makes it easier for us to discover our own gifts and develop them more swiftly for the Lord's use. So I share these thoughts with you, not as the final word on the matter, but as a study which I believe will be helpful to you in becoming the effective instrument Christ desires you to be in his Kingdom.

Evidence of Categories. The original Greek words used in the Bible to describe the various gifts offer much justification for the division of gifts into the categories I use.

Charismaton, the word used in 1 Corinthians 12:4, means "gift of grace." Grace, in one sense, is the power of God working through the believer to accomplish God's will and purpose. Used in relation to gifts, it refers to the basic inward drive that God places in each believer as a means of expressing his divine love. The word "motivation" encompasses the various shades of meaning presented by *charismaton* as well as any word the English language offers.

Diakonion, the Greek word used in 1 Corinthians 12:5, refers to the opportunities of Christian service available to us for the exercise of our basic motivation. "Ministries" is the best English word to describe it.

Enegema phanerosis, the Greek term found in 1 Corinthians 12:6, denotes the result produced in the lives of others as we use our spiritual gifts. "Manifestations" seems an adequate English rendering of this term.

A Note of Caution. To summarize the categories, then, there are:

1. *Motivations*—the basic inward drive God places in us.
2. *Ministries*—the opportunities for Christian service God makes available to us for the exercise of our motivations.
3. *Manifestations*—the results God brings forth in the lives of others as we exercise our motivations through our ministries.

Our goal should not be to seek manifestations— that is, to see certain results from the exercise of our gifts. Rather, we should seek to determine what our motivational gift is and then find the most effective ministry for expressing it.

The Bible lists seven motivational gifts. They are:

> Prophecy
> Service
> Teaching
> Exhortation
> Giving
> Administration (organization or ruling)
> Mercy

Ten ministries are listed:

> Apostle
> Prophet
> Evangelist
> Pastor
> Teacher
> Worker of power
> Healing
> Helper
> Administration
> Tongues

The manifestations mentioned are:

> Word of wisdom
> Knowledge
> Faith
> Healings
> Word of prophecy
> Miracles
> Discerning spirit
> Interpreter of tongues
> Various tongues

MOTIVATIONAL GIFTS

First, we should discover, with the help of the Holy Spirit, what our basic motivational gift is. Then we should concentrate on performing the ministry or ministries through which that particular motivational gift can be exercised. The manifestations, or results, we simply leave to the Lord. He determines who is benefited by the exercise of our gifts and in what ways. We don't have to be concerned about that.

To discover your motivational gift, you need to understand the meaning of each such gift, the qualities that usually go with it, and some of the ways in which the gift can be misused. Here are the definitions and qualities of each gift and a list of some of the dangers of misuse.

Prophecy.

Definition—   Proclaiming spiritual truth; presenting God's truth so that unrighteous motives or actions are revealed and God's plan of salvation is set forth clearly and simply.

Qualities—   Ability to be persuasive in speech, to bring to light things previously concealed or not understood, to reveal to men the secrets of their hearts, causing them to turn to God (1 Corinthians 14:25). A prophet, or proclaimer, must (1) have love without hypocrisy, (2) despise that which is evil, (3) grasp that which is good.

Misuses—   Being proud of eloquence and persuasiveness; being more dependent on speaking ability than on the power of the Holy Spirit to bring conviction; seeing people as groups rather than as individuals with personal needs.

Serving.

Definition—   Demonstrating love by meeting practical needs of others.

Qualities—   Ability to detect personal
needs, to overlook personal discomfort
in order to meet these needs. A server
must (1) have genuine affection for
others, (2) demonstrate brotherly responsibility, (3) be willing to let others
have the credit for service he has done.

Misuses—   Being so busy trying to meet
others' physical needs that spiritual needs are somewhat minimized
or neglected; usually serving those
who can best "return the favor";
spending so much time helping others
that one's own spiritual life and needs
are not cared for properly.

Teaching.

Definition—   Systematically researching and presenting the truths of God's Word.

Qualities—   Ability to share biblical principles with others in an interesting,
practical manner. A teacher must (1) be
willing to apply what he learns to his
own life before passing it on to others,
(2) be orderly and systematic in his
own study and in his teaching, and (3)
constantly check his material to make
sure he is presenting biblical truth
accurately.

Misuses—   Boasting of the knowledge he has acquired; concentrating on details of information rather than communicating basic life principles; being more concerned about the research than the response of his students (in other words, boring).

Exhortation.
Definition— Stimulating and nurturing the faith of others.

Qualities—   Ability to urge others to adopt a course of conduct; ability to provide counseling that results in spiritual growth, that enables others to put biblical principles into everyday life. An exhorter must (1) rejoice in expectations concerning others, (2) be patient with slow progress, (3) be persistent in prayer.

Misuses—   Boasting of personal results in counseling of others; becoming discouraged when the counseled person's growth is slow; motivating others for selfish reason; devoting too much time to those who want only temporary relief from problems rather than lasting spiritual progress.

Giving.
Definition— Entrusting personal assets to others for the support of their ministry.

Qualities—   Ability to organize personal business in order to gain assets; ability to make quick decisions regarding the material needs of others; unusual discernment concerning worthiness of other persons' ministries. The giver must (1) give freely to the total needs of fellow Christians, (2) take a genuine interest in the needs of strangers.

Misuses— Being proud of generosity in giving; measuring spiritual success in terms of material assets; overlooking long-range goals in meeting immediate needs.

Administration (Ruling or Organization).
Definition— Coordinating the activities of yourself and others for the attainment of common goals.

Qualities— Ability to preside over operations, to lead, to stand before others; ability to distinguish major objectives and help others visualize them. A ruler must (1) bless those who curse him, (2) do whatever he can to make the lives of others happy and spiritually prosperous.

Misuses— Being proud of power over others; using people to achieve personal goals instead of meeting their personal needs; overlooking major character faults in those who are useful to the ruler in reaching his goals.

Mercy.
Definition— Identifying with and comforting those who are in distress.

Qualities— Ability to feel empathy with the misfortunes and miseries of others;

ability to relate mentally and emotionally with others' needs and to give them aid. One having the gift of mercy must (1) share the happiness of those who are happy, (2) enter into the grief of those who are in sorrow.

Misuses— Being proud of ability to empathize; resenting others who are not sensitive to personal needs of people; failure to be firm with people who have problems when firmness would help them more than sympathy; being guided too much by emotions, not enough by logic.

GUIDE TO MOTIVATIONAL GIFTS

Persons possessing each of the motivational gifts tend to display certain identifiable traits in their lives. A listing of the most recognizable of these chracteristics has been compiled. This listing has been a tremendous help to many people in discovering their spiritual gifts.

To use the list, simply go over the characteristics given for each motivational gift, devoting careful thought and prayer to each characteristic. If you find that several of the characteristics of a particular gift match up with traits in your own personality, this is a good indication that that gift is one the Holy Spirit has given you.

You will also find listed some misunderstandings people may have concerning persons with each gift.

Ponder the lists prayerfully. You may very well be on the threshold of making the exciting discovery of your spiritual gift or gifts.

Characteristics of Prophecy.
1. A need to express the message verbally.

2. The ability to discern the character and motives of people. (2 Peter 2:1-3)

3. The ability to identify, define, and hate evil. (Romans 12:9; 1 Timothy 3:7)

4. Willingness to experience brokenness in order to prompt brokenness in others. (John 20:21)

5. Dependence on scriptural truth to validate his authority. (1 Peter 4:11)

6. A desire for outward evidences as proof of inward conviction. (1 Corinthians 14:25)

7. Directness, frankness, and persuasiveness in speaking. (Titus 2:6)

8. A concern for the reputation and program of God. (2 Samuel 12:14)

9. An inward weeping and personal identification with the sins of those he speaks to.

10. An eagerness to have others point out his blind spot (spiritual flaw he is not aware of), so he can teach others about his flaw and see them repent. (Psalm 51)

Misunderstandings.
1. Frankness may be viewed as harshness.

2. Interest in groups may be interpreted as lack of interest in individuals.

3. Efforts to gain results may be seen as use of gimmicks.

4. Focus on right and wrong may be judged as intolerance of anything less than perfection.

5. Emphasis on decisions for Christ may appear as neglect of spiritual growth.

6. Public boldness and strict standards may hinder intimate relationships with others.

7. The strong desire to convey truth may be interpreted as unwillingness to listen to another's point of view.

Characteristics of Serving.
1. Ability to recall specific likes and dislikes of people.

2. Alertness to detect and meet practical needs, especially those requiring manual projects.

3. Eagerness to meet needs as quickly as possible.

4. Physical stamina to fulfill needs with disregard for weariness.

5. Willingness to use personal funds.

6. Desire to sense sincere appreciation, and ability to detect insincerity.

7. Desire to complete a project, leaving evidence of having done more than was expected.

8. Involvement in a variety of activities with a seeming inability to say "no."

9. Greater enjoyment of short-range goals; frustration over long-range projects.

10. Frustration when limitations of time are attached to jobs (prefers to work on own schedule).

Misunderstandings.
1. Quickness in meeting needs may appear to be pushiness.

2. Attempts to complete projects quickly may cause some to feel excluded from jobs.

3. Busyness in meeting others' needs may seem to be neglect of own family.

4. Eagerness in serving may prompt others to suspect motive is self-gain.

5. May seem to resent others who do not detect and meet obvious needs.

6. Insistence on serving may appear to be rejection of service offered by others.

7. Desire to sense sincere appreciation may make one appear to be easily hurt.

8. Quickness in meeting needs may interfere with spiritual lessons God is teaching others through their needs.

9. Meeting practical needs may be judged as lack of interest in spiritual matters.

10. Stamina may be interpreted as insensitivity or impatience with others.

11. Success with short-range goals may result in promotion to leadership positions, bringing frustration or disorganization because of long-range objectives accompanying these positions.

12. Inability to ignore others' needs may result in being sidetracked from employer's instructions.

Characteristics of Teaching.
1. Belief that this gift is foundational to other gifts.

2. Emphasis on the accuracy of words.

3. Testing of the knowledge of others who teach.

4. Delight in research in order to validate truth.

5. Validating of new information by established systems of truth.

6. Presentation of truth in a systematic sequence.

7. Avoidance of illustrations from non-biblical sources.

8. Resistance to scriptural illustrations out of context.

9. Greater joy in researching truth than presenting it.

Misunderstandings.
1. Emphasis on accuracy of scriptural interpretation may appear to be neglect of its practical application.

2. Others' research may appear to depend on more than the teaching ministry of the Holy Spirit through meditation and thus be more sensible or applicable.

3. Use of knowledge in testing others may appear to be pride of learning.

4. Concern to impart details of research may appear to be unnecessary to listeners.

5. Need to be objective in research may appear to reveal lack of warmth and feeling.

Characteristics of Exhortation.
1. Desire to visualize specific achievement and prescribe steps of action.

2. Tendency to avoid systems of information which lack practical application.

3. Ability to see how tribulation can produce new levels of maturity.

4. Dependence on visible acceptance when speaking to individuals or groups.

5. Discovery of insights from human experience which can be validated and amplified in Scripture.

6. Enjoyment in seeing others eager to follow steps of action.

7. Grief if teaching is not accompanied by practical steps of action.

8. Delight in personal conferences that result in new insights for helping others grow spiritually.

Misunderstandings.
1. Emphasis on steps of action may appear to be oversimplification of problem.

2. Urgency in giving steps of action may appear as overconfidence in value of advice.

3. Desire to win non-Christians through living examples may appear to be lack of interest in personal evangelism.

4. Use of Scripture for practical application may appear to take it out of context.

5. Emphasis on steps of action may appear to be a disregard for feelings of those being counseled.

Characteristics of Giving.
1. Ability to make wise purchases and investments.

2. Desire to give quietly to effective projects or ministries (avoiding publicity).

3. Tendency to use giving to motivate others to give.

4. Alertness to valid needs; fear that others may overlook these needs.

5. Enjoyment in meeting needs without the pressure of appeals.

6. Joy when a gift proves to be an answer to a specific prayer.

7. Dependency on marriage partner's counsel to confirm amount of a gift.

8. Concern that the gift be of high quality.

9. Desire to feel a part of the work of person or organization to whom gift is made.

Misunderstandings.
1. Need to deal with large sums of money may appear as focus on temporal values.

2. Desire to increase the effectiveness of a ministry by giving may appear as an attempt to control the work of person to whom gift is made.

3. Attempt to encourage others to give may appear as lack of generosity and unnecessary pressure.

4. Lack of response to pressure appeals may appear as lack of generosity.

5. Personal frugality may appear to friends and relatives as selfishness with regard to their wants.

Characteristics of Administration (ruling or organizing).
1. Ability to see the overall picture and to clarify long-range goals.

2. Capacity for organizing that for which he is responsible.

3. Desire to complete tasks as quickly as possible.

4. Awareness of resources available to complete a task.

5. Ability to know what can or cannot be delegated.

6. Tendency to stand aside until those in charge turn over responsibility to him.

7. Tendency to assume responsibility if no structured leadership exists.

8. Willingness to endure reaction from workers in order to accomplish the ultimate task.

9. Fulfillment in seeing all pieces coming together and others enjoying finished product.

10. Desire to move on to new challenge when task at hand is fully complete.

Misunderstandings.

1. Ability to delegate responsibility may appear as laziness or attempt to avoid work.

2. Willingness to endure negative reaction to his plans may appear as callousness toward others.

3. Neglect in explaining why tasks must be done may prompt workers to feel they are being used for his personal gain.

4. Viewing of people as resources may cause others to feel he regards projects as more important than people.

5. Desire to complete tasks swiftly may appear to be insensitivity to the schedule or to weariness or priorities of workers.

Characteristics of Mercy.

1. Ability to sense an atmosphere of joy or distress in an individual or group.

2. Attraction to and understanding of people who are in distress.

3. Desire to remove hurts and bring healing to others.

4. Greater concern for mental distress than physical distress.

5. Avoidance of firmness unless way in which it will benefit is obvious.

6. Sensitivity to words and actions which will hurt other people.

7. Ability to discern sincere motives in other people.

8. Enjoyment and unity with those who are sensitive to the needs and feelings of others.

9. Tendency to shut out or avoid those who are insincere or insensitive.

Misunderstandings.

1. Avoiding of firmness may appear to be weakness and indecisiveness.

2. Sensitivity to the spirit and feelings of others may cause some to feel that emotions, rather than logic, are providing directions.

3. Attraction to and understanding of those in distress may be misinterpreted by persons of opposite sex as physical attraction.

4. Sensitivity to words and actions which cause hurts may appear to be effort to take up other people's offenses.

5. Ability to detect insincere motives may cause some to feel person with gift of mercy is hard to get to know.

SELF-TEST ON SPIRITUAL GIFTS

By now you may have narrowed your decision down to two gifts. Characteristics of some of the gifts are a little hard to distinguish from each other. If you are stuck on a choice of two gifts with similar characteristics, the following self-test may help you.

PROPHECY OR TEACHING: If you were limited to either doing research for a lesson or presenting the lesson, which would you prefer?

RESEARCH?—Then your primary gift is probably teaching.
PRESENTING?—Then your gift is probably prophecy.

PROPHECY OR EXHORTATION: Do you enjoy speaking more to a group or to an individual?

GROUP?—Prophecy.
INDIVIDUAL?—Exhortation.

SERVING OR MERCY: Are you more comfortable in helping meet the practical needs of others or in meeting their mental and emotional needs?

PRACTICAL NEEDS?—Serving.
EMOTIONAL NEEDS?—Mercy.

TEACHING OR MERCY: Are you more concerned with the atmosphere of a worship service or the scriptural pattern of the service?

ATMOSPHERE?—Mercy.
SCRIPTURAL PATTERN?—Teaching.

SERVING OR RULING: If you were given the responsibility to organize for an activity, would you prefer delegating the responsibility to others or performing most of the task yourself?

DELEGATING?—Ruling.
PERFORMING YOURSELF?—Serving.

SERVING OR EXHORTATION: Do you enjoy counseling an individual in order to give the person steps of action or in order to discern what the practical needs are and how to meet those needs?

STEPS OF ACTION?—Exhorter.
PRACTICAL NEEDS?—Serving.

TEACHING OR EXHORTATION: Do you have a present ministry of teaching? If so, do you enjoy teaching in order to participate in research or as an opportunity to counsel others?

RESEARCH?—Teaching.
COUNSEL?—Exhorter.

EXHORTATION OR RULING: If you were head of an organization, would you solve conflicts by changing an employee's position in the organization or by focusing on changing the employee's attitude?

> CHANGE POSITION?—Ruling.
> CHANGE ATTITUDE?—Exhorter.

GIVING OR SERVING: Do you receive greater joy in giving to meet the practical needs of an individual or in giving to aid someone's specific ministry to others?

> PRACTICAL NEEDS?—Serving.
> MINISTRY TO OTHERS?—Giving.

EXHORTATION OR MERCY: Which is more important to you, spiritual healing or spiritual growth? If healing, is it healing for the sake of preventing suffering or to challenge one to spiritual growth?

> PREVENT SUFFERING?—Mercy.
> CHALLENGE TO GROWTH?—Exhortation.
> END SUFFERING?—Mercy.

RULING OR MERCY: Do you desire harmony in an organization in order that it may run smoothly or because of the joy and fellowship that results in oneness of spirit?

> RUN SMOOTHLY?—Ruling.
> ONENESS?—Mercy.

MERCY OR TEACHING: Are you motivated to do research in order to establish correct doctrine or in order to understand doctrinal differences among Christians and learn how to bring harmony and oneness?

> DOCTRINE?—Teaching.
> HARMONY?—Mercy.

MINISTRIES AND MANIFESTATIONS

Once you have determined your motivational gift, the basic spiritual drive the Lord has given you, then you need to think about that gift in relation to ministries and manifestations. As I mentioned before, motivational gifts are exercised through the various ministries. Then God brings forth the manifestations in others according to his desires and purposes.

Ministry Gifts. First, some capsule definitions. The ministries are:

1. Apostle—one sent forth for special Christian service.

2. Prophet—a proclaimer of God's message, primarily among Christians.

3. Evangelist—a proclaimer of God's message, primarily to non-Christians.

4. Pastor—one who oversees and cares for the needs of Christians.

5. Teacher—one who clarifies and preserves truth.

6. Worker of power—one who performs supernatural deeds.

7. Healing—one who exercises the gift of healing.

8. Helper—one who assists leadership to minister to the weak and needy.

9. Administrator—one who guides and directs the local church.

10. Tongues—speaker of various tongues.

You may have discovered that your motivational gift is exhortation. If so, you may choose several ministries—or God may open opportunities to you through several ministries—to exercise that gift. You could exercise it as an apostle, prophet, evangelist, pastor, teacher, or perhaps one or more of the other ministries. As you exercise your gift, God would use your service to produce benefits or manifestations that he desires to be produced in others. And in a group of people exposed to your ministry, he might well produce different manifestations in different persons.

Manifestation Gifts. Suppose, for example, that you exercise your gift of exhortation through the ministry of prophecy—that is, as a prophet, one who proclaims God's message primarily to Christians. And suppose in your message to a group of

Christians, you encourage your hearers to gain a clearer conscience.

Using your message—or his message as delivered by you—God might produce in your listeners all of the manifestations listed in the Bible, meting them out in this manner:

1. Word of wisdom—One might see forgiveness from God's point of view.

2. Word of knowledge—Another might understand how to gain a clear conscience.

3. Faith—Another might be moved to a deeper dependence regarding a clear conscience.

4. Healing—Another might gain health as he applies this truth to his life.

5. Effective miracles—Another might allow God to work supernaturally through gaining a clear conscience.

6. Prophecy—Another might have hidden areas of his life brought to the light of his attention.

7. Distinguishing of spirits—Another might discern attitudes which would hinder him in seeking forgiveness.

8. Various tongues—Another's spirit might be freed to communicate with God.

9. Interpretation of tongues—Another might be given a translation of spiritual truth.

HINDRANCES TO GIFT DISCOVERY

If you have not yet determined what your motivation gift is, go back over the characteristics and prayerfully consider them again. Seek the help and advice of other Christians, especially your pastor and others who appear to be leading mature, fulfilling, and fruitful Christian lives. The Lord may be able to use these other Christians to help you discover your spiritual gift(s) and the ministries through which the Lord might enable you to use it.

If you still have trouble, it is possible that it is because of one or more of several factors that sometimes hinder people in their effort to discover their spiritual gift. Here are a few such factors:

Unresolved root problems in personal living. It is significant that the gifts of Romans 12 are not mentioned until the moral conflicts of Romans 1—11 are dealt with.

Lack of involvement with the needs of others. Our gifts are stirred up and discovered as we focus on the needs of others rather than on what our ministry is to be. A servant's heart is essential in discovering your spiritual gift.

Attempts to imitate motivational gifts of others. If a Christian is caught up in trying to imitate other Christians, he will not be free to discover his own gift.

Failure to analyze why certain activities appeal to us. It is important for us to understand what the basic motivation is for our present Christian activities. Many activities can be the means of fulfilling our basic motivation.

Confusion between motivational gift and ministry gift. A person with the motivation of teaching may, for example, have a ministry of prophecy which he thoroughly enjoys. This may cause him to question which one is his actual motivational gift.

Understanding your motivational gift and the characteristics of the gifts of others will help you to understand why you and others have the different interests you have.

Knowing your spiritual gift also will help you to be effective in your service for the Lord without ruining your physical or emotional health. Exercising your own gift through the power of the Holy Spirit, and not trying to imitate others or perform spiritual services with mere human power and wisdom, will enable you to serve with a minimum of weariness and stress and with a maximum of effectiveness.

GOD'S EXCITING PLAN

This is God's exciting, effective plan for your fulfillment and for the building up of the body of Christ, the church. It is a plan that offers reward and fulfillment for the individual believer and harmony among the body of believers.

Ignoring and neglecting this plan has cost the church, and individual Christians, much in happiness and fruitfulness. I pray that you will not abandon your quest to discover and develop your spiritual gift until God has rewarded you with thrilling success. And once you have found your gift, I pray that you will then dedicate yourself to helping other Christians make the same exciting discovery you have made.

THIRTY-FIVE years ago, a boy was born in the charity ward of a Texas hospital. Three weeks later his divorced and impoverished mother placed an ad in a local newspaper offering him to someone who would give him love and a home. The odds are about a thousand to one against a boy like that making it in life, but the child who grew up to become evangelist James Robison not only has changed his personal destiny, but is helping millions of all ages, from all walks of life, to trade in their own troubled existences for lives of inner peace through Jesus Christ.

Responding to the newspaper ad, Rev. and Mrs. H.D. Hale of Pasadena, Texas, brought James into their home where he lived for the first five years of his life. He then spent ten years in Austin with his mother during difficult years upset by a stepfather who had become an alcoholic.

With his mother's permission, James re-

turned to live with the Hales and finish high
school where he played for two years on the
school's varsity football team. On an earlier
visit to their home he had committed his life
to Jesus Christ at Memorial Baptist Church in
Pasadena. It was a sincere, though unspec-
tacular commitment. Three years later, when
James was eighteen, Jesus Christ . . .

CLASS 242.1
Rob
ACC

Robison, Jwmes
(LAST NAME OF AUTHOR)

New Growth**Holy Spirit
(BOOK TITLE)

DATE DUE | ISSUED TO

242.1
Rob

CLASS | ACC.

Robinson, James
(LAST NAME OF AUTHOR)

New Growth**Holy Spirit
(BOOK TITLE)

PARK CITY BAPTIST CHURCH
PARK CITY, KENTUCKY
STAMP LIBRARY OWNERSHIP

CODE 4386-03   BROADMAN SUPPLIES
CLS-3   MADE IN U.S.A.

times are desperate—that I must warn the
people, and that I must not—and will not—
compromise His Word!"